Developing Android Applications
with Flex 4.5

Developing Android Applications
with Flex 4.5

Rich Tretola

Beijing · Cambridge · Farnham · Köln · Sebastopol · Tokyo

Developing Android Applications with Flex 4.5
by Rich Tretola

Copyright © 2011 Rich Tretola. All rights reserved.
Printed in the United States of America.

Published by O'Reilly Media, Inc., 1005 Gravenstein Highway North, Sebastopol, CA 95472.

O'Reilly books may be purchased for educational, business, or sales promotional use. Online editions are also available for most titles (*http://my.safaribooksonline.com*). For more information, contact our corporate/institutional sales department: (800) 998-9938 or *corporate@oreilly.com*.

Editor: Mary Treseler	**Cover Designer:** Karen Montgomery
Production Editor: Kristen Borg	**Interior Designer:** David Futato
Proofreader: O'Reilly Production Services	**Illustrator:** Robert Romano

Printing History:

May 2011:	First Edition.

ISBN: 978-1-449-30537-6

[LSI]

1304349936

Table of Contents

Preface

Introduction to Android

The Android mobile operating system was first introduced in the fall of 2008 as part of the G1 handset. Android began to gain some momentum as major device manufactures like Motorola, HTC, Sony, and Samsung adopted Android to run on their hardware. As the number of available devices began to grow (allowing mobile customers a wide range of choices), the number of Android handsets being activated each day increased dramatically. Android's operating system continued to evolve through versions 1.0, 1.5, 1.6, 2.0, 2.1—and then 2.2, which was the point at which Adobe AIR became available within the Android market. The number of Android devices running 2.2 or higher continues to grow, which means that the user base for applications based on the methods discussed in this book is also expanding.

This book will walk you through the creation of your first Adobe AIR application using the Flex 4.5 framework, and provides examples of how to interact with the device's many components and features. These include GPS, the camera, the gallery, the accelerometer, the multitouch display, the `StageWebView`, operating system interactions, and more.

Who This Book Is For

Developing Android Applications with Adobe Flex 4.5 is a book targeting all levels of developers. It starts with a basic Hello World application and then quickly moves to more complicated examples where the Android APIs are explored.

Who This Book Is Not For

This book is not for developers who are interested in developing native Android applications with Java. This book will only provide examples of Android application development using Adobe Flex 4.5 and ActionScript 3.

Conventions Used in This Book

The following typographical conventions are used in this book:

Menu options
> Menu options are shown using the → character, such as File→Open.

Italic
> Indicates new terms, URLs, email addresses, filenames, and file extensions.

`Constant width`
> This is used for program listings, as well as within paragraphs, to refer to program elements such as variable or function names, databases, data types, environment variables, statements, and keywords.

`Constant width bold`
> This shows commands or other text that should be typed literally by the developer.

`Constant width italic`
> This shows text that should be replaced with user-supplied values or by values determined by context.

This Book's Example Files

You can download the example files for this book from this location:

> *http://oreilly.com/catalog/9781449305376*

Where necessary, multiple code samples are provided for each recipe to correspond with different development environments. Each sample will be separated into a folder for the specific environment. Each application should include the necessary code for your environment, as well as an application descriptor file.

Using Code Examples

This book is here to help you get your job done. In general, you may use the code in this book in your programs and documentation. You do not need to contact us for permission unless you're reproducing a significant portion of the code. For example, writing a program that uses several chunks of code from this book does not require permission. Selling or distributing a CD-ROM of examples from O'Reilly books does require permission. Answering a question by citing this book and quoting example code does not require permission. Incorporating a significant amount of example code from this book into your product's documentation does require permission.

We appreciate, but do not require, attribution. An attribution usually includes the title, author, publisher, and ISBN. For example: "*Developing Android Applications with Flex 4.5* by Rich Tretola (O'Reilly). Copyright 2011 Rich Tretola, 978-1-449-30537-6."

If you feel your use of code examples falls outside fair use or the permission given above, feel free to contact us at *permissions@oreilly.com*.

How to Use This Book

Development rarely happens in a vacuum. In today's world, email, Twitter, blog posts, coworkers, friends, and colleagues all play a vital role in helping you solve development problems. Consider this book yet another resource at your disposal to help you solve the snags you will encounter when developing an application. The content is arranged in such a way that solutions should be easy to find and easy to understand. And this book does have another big advantage: it is available any time of the day or night.

Safari® Books Online

Safari Safari Books Online is an on-demand digital library that lets you easily search over 7,500 technology and creative reference books and videos to find the answers you need quickly.

With a subscription, you can read any page and watch any video from our library online. Read books on your cell phone and mobile devices. Access new titles before they are available for print, and get exclusive access to manuscripts in development and post feedback for the authors. Copy and paste code samples, organize your favorites, download chapters, bookmark key sections, create notes, print out pages, and benefit from tons of other time-saving features.

O'Reilly Media has uploaded this book to the Safari Books Online service. To have full digital access to this book and others on similar topics from O'Reilly and other publishers, sign up for free at *http://my.safaribooksonline.com*.

How to Contact Us

Please address comments and questions concerning this book to the publisher:

> O'Reilly Media, Inc.
> 1005 Gravenstein Highway North
> Sebastopol, CA 95472
> 800-998-9938 (in the United States or Canada)
> 707-829-0515 (international or local)
> 707-829-0104 (fax)

We have a web page for this book, where we list errata, examples, and any additional information. You can access this page at:

> *http://oreilly.com/catalog/0636920020172/*

To comment or ask technical questions about this book, send email to:

bookquestions@oreilly.com

For more information about our books, courses, conferences, and news, see our website at *http://www.oreilly.com.*

Find us on Facebook: *http://facebook.com/oreilly*

Follow us on Twitter: *http://twitter.com/oreillymedia*

Watch us on YouTube: *http://www.youtube.com/oreillymedia*

Acknowledgments

First and foremost, I would like to thank my wife and best friend Kim, and my daughters Skye, Coral, and Trinity for their love and support. I love you all!

I would like to say thank to the Adobe Flex team and the members of the Flex CAB who provided early access and support to the AIR 2.6 and Flash Builder 4.5 tools and documentation.

Thank you as well to Mary Treseler from O'Reilly for providing this opportunity.

CHAPTER 1

Hello World

This section will walk you through building your first AIR on Android application using Adobe Flash Builder 4.5. If you don't have Flash Builder 4.5, you can get a trial version from Adobe at *http://www.adobe.com/products/flashbuilder/*.

Now that you have Flash Builder 4.5 installed, open it, and let's get started.

Create a Flex Mobile Project

Create a new Flex Mobile Project by choosing File→New→Flex Mobile Project, as shown in Figure 1-1.

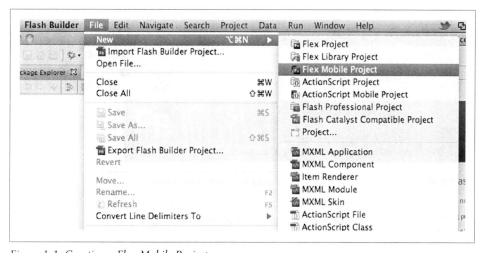

Figure 1-1. Creating a Flex Mobile Project

This will open the New Flex Mobile Project wizard, which will walk you through the rest of the project creation process. The first screen you are presented with will allow you to set the project name, location, and Flex SDK. Enter the name *HelloWorld* as the project name, and leave the other settings on their defaults. Click Next, as shown in Figure 1-2.

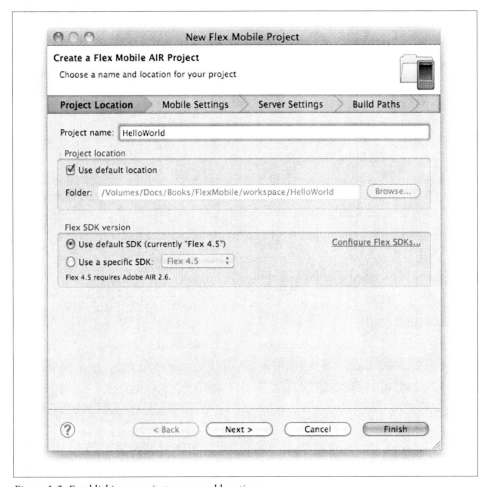

Figure 1-2. Establishing a project name and location

The second screen in the new project wizard is where you can select settings specific to the target platform. Unless you have installed a plug-in to add additional platforms, you will only have one option—Google Android, which is already selected as the target platform. Google Android gives you the option of three different application types, which are Blank, View-Based Application, or Tabbed Application. For this first project, please select View-Based Application, as shown in Figure 1-3, and leave the other settings on their defaults.

Next, click on the Permissions tab. Within this tab, you will be able to select the permissions that your application will need in order to interact with the native Android

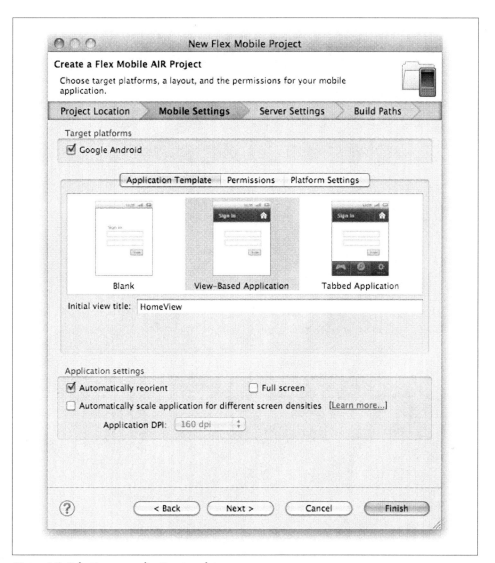

Figure 1-3. Selecting an application template

APIs. Please be sure to only select the permissions that apply to your application, as once your application is uploaded to the Android Market, these permissions will be used to filter the devices that will be able to install your application. For example, if you select Camera as a required permission and your application doesn't actually use a camera, any Android device that doesn't have a camera will never be able to install your application. For the purposes of this exercise, leave only the INTERNET permission selected, as shown in Figure 1-4. Click Next.

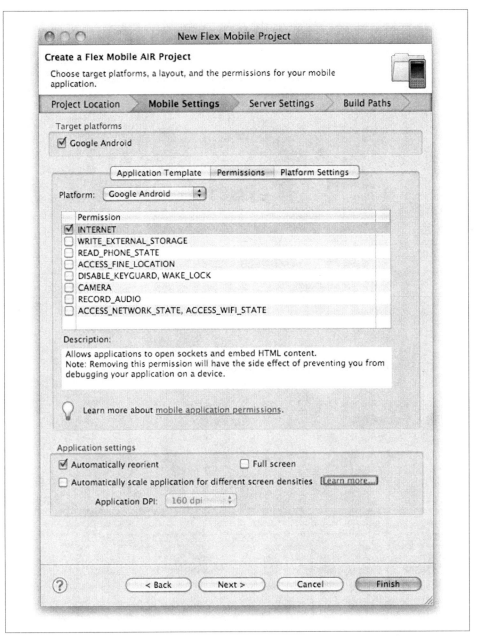

Figure 1-4. Setting Android permissions

The next screen allows for the configuration of an application server and output folder. For this project we will not be using an application server, so leave it set to None/Other, and click Next as shown in Figure 1-5.

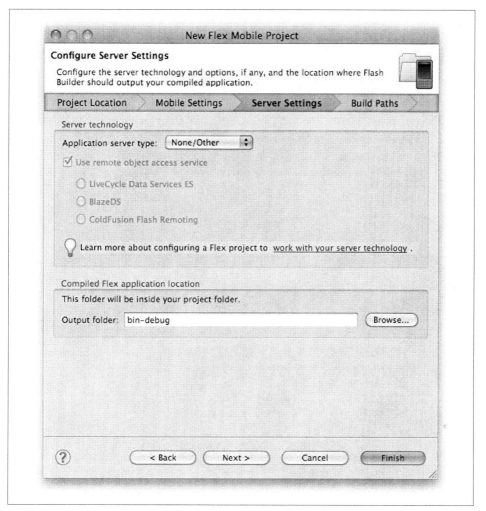

Figure 1-5. The Server Settings screen

The last screen that you will see in the wizard is the Build Paths screen, where you will be able to set your Application ID. This setting is very important, as Google uses this to identify your application in the Android Market. To ensure that your application has a unique identifier, the reverse domain naming convention works best. Figure 1-6 shows the value of *com.domain.mobile.HelloWorld* as the application ID. By replacing the word *domain* with a domain that you own, you can ensure that your application ID is unique. Complete this step and click Finish.

Flash Builder will now create your new project, and by default, *HelloWorldHomeView.mxml* will be created and opened in the workspace along with the *HelloWorld.mxml* main application file. This is shown in Figure 1-7.

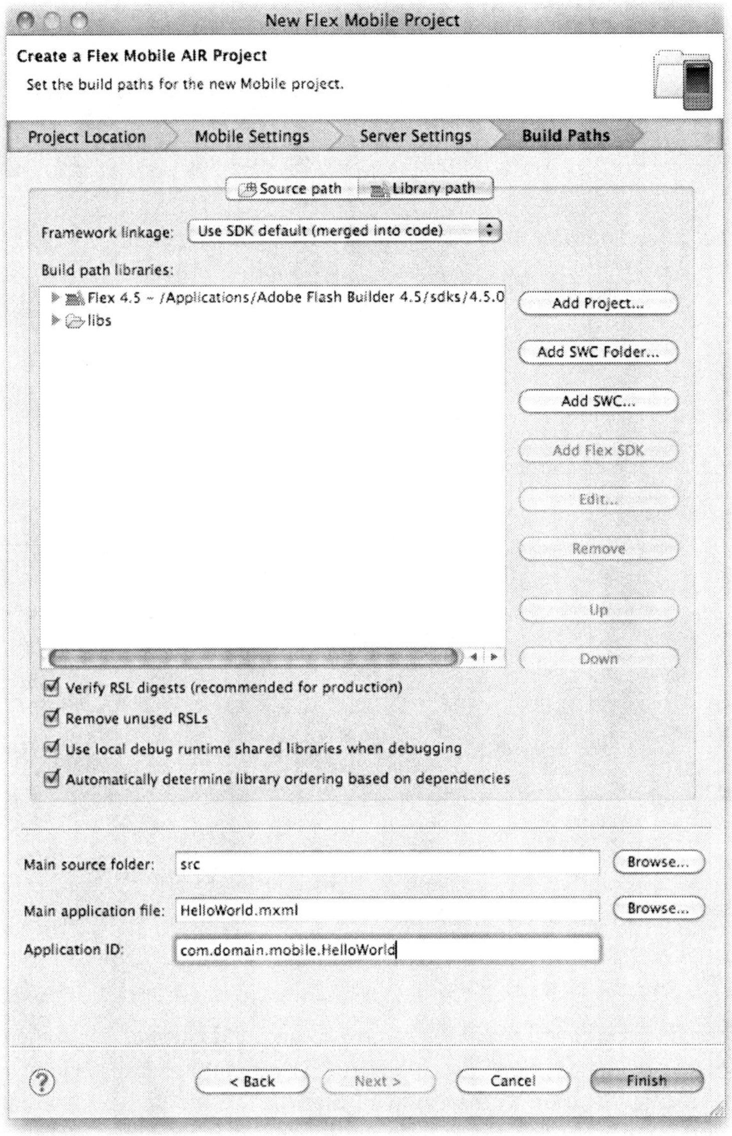

Figure 1-6. Adding an Application ID

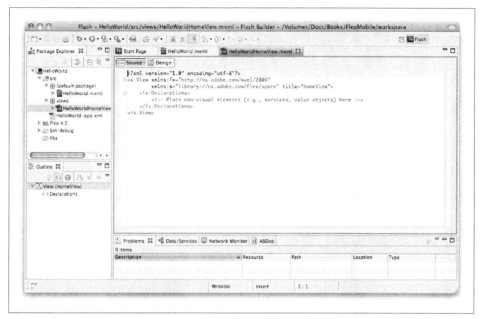

Figure 1-7. A new project has been created

Let's update the contents of *HelloWorldHomeView.mxml* by adding a Label:

```xml
<?xml version="1.0" encoding="utf-8"?>
<s:View xmlns:fx="http://ns.adobe.com/mxml/2009"
        xmlns:s="library://ns.adobe.com/flex/spark" title="HomeView">
    <fx:Declarations>
        <!-- Place non-visual elements (e.g., services, value objects) here -->
    </fx:Declarations>

    <s:Label text="Hello World" fontSize="24"
            horizontalCenter="0" verticalCenter="0"/>

</s:View>
```

Now we can run the application. To do this, right-click on the *HelloWorld.mxml* file within the Package Explorer and select Run As→Mobile Application, as shown in Figure 1-8. Since this is our first time running this application, the Run Configurations window will open. To run this using the Flash builder emulator, select "On desktop" as the Launch method and select a device from the drop-down menu, as shown in Figure 1-9.

If you have an Android device, you can plug it into a USB port and select "On device" to run the Hello World application on your phone.

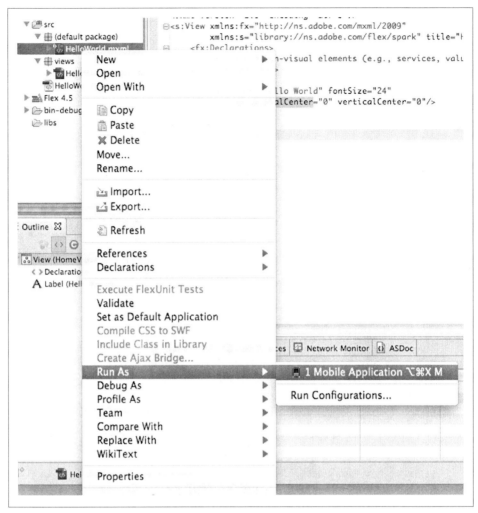

Figure 1-8. Running an application on a mobile device

Now click Apply, and then click Run—you will see the Hello World application launch within the desktop simulator or on the device. Figure 1-10 shows Hello World running on a device.

Congratulations: you have just created your first AIR on Android application with Adobe Flex 4.5.

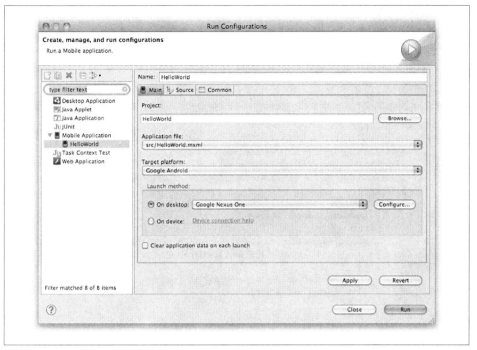

Figure 1-9. The Run Configurations window

Figure 1-10. The Hello World application in action

Debug a Flex Mobile Project

Now that you have created your Hello World application and ran it using the Run Configurations window, you may wish to debug your application. Fortunately for you, the workflow for debugging a Flex Mobile application is the same as debugging any other Adobe Flex or Adobe AIR application.

Update the *HelloWorld.mxml* file to include a *creationComplete* handler as shown here:

```
<?xml version="1.0" encoding="utf-8"?>
<s:ViewNavigatorApplicationxmlns:fx="http://ns.adobe.com/mxml/2009"
        xmlns:s="library://ns.adobe.com/flex/spark"
        firstView="views.HelloWorldHomeView"
        creationComplete="viewnavigatorapplication1_creationCompleteHandler(event)">
    <fx:Script>
        <![CDATA[
            importmx.events.FlexEvent;

            protectedfunction viewnavigatorapplication1_creationCompleteHandler
                    (event:FlexEvent):void
            {
                // TODO Auto-generated method stub
                trace("hello world");
            }

        ]]>
    </fx:Script>
    <fx:Declarations>
        <!-- Place non-visual elements (e.g., services, value objects) here -->
    </fx:Declarations>
</s:ViewNavigatorApplication>
```

We now need to toggle a breakpoint within the application on line 14, to demonstrate a debugging session. To do this, right-click on line 14 within Flash Builder and select Toggle Breakpoint from the context menu. Figure 1-11 shows this process. A small blue dot will appear in the gutter, showing that the break point is enabled.

We are now ready to debug this application. To do this, right-click on the *Hello-World.mxml* file within Package Explorer and select Debug As→Mobile Application, as shown in Figure 1-12. Since this is our first time debugging this application, the Debug Configurations window will open. To debug this using the Flash builder emulator, select "On desktop" as the Launch method and select a device from the drop-down menu, as shown in Figure 1-13.

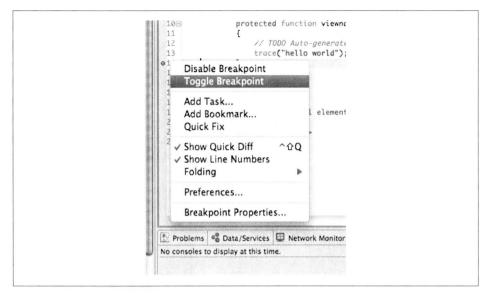

Figure 1-11. Toggling a breakpoint

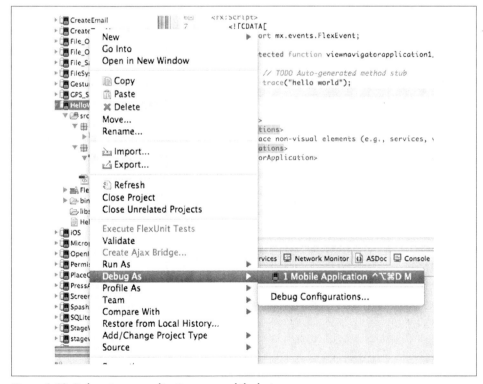

Figure 1-12. Debugging an application on a mobile device

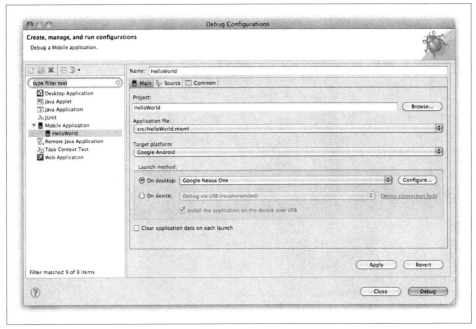

Figure 1-13. The Debug Configurations window

 As mentioned earlier, if you have an Android device, you can plug it into your USB port and select "On device" to debug the Hello World application on your phone.

When asked if you would like to switch to the Flash Builder debug perspective, select "Yes" (see Figure 1-14). Figure 1-15 shows the application paused on line 14 within Flash Builder's debug perspective. You can see the trace message within the console panel. To allow the application to complete, click the Resume button.

Congratulations: you have just completed your first Flash Builder debug session for a Flex Mobile application.

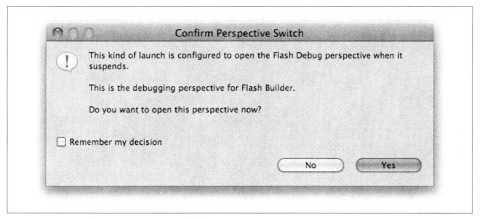

Figure 1-14. Confirming the switch to debug perspective

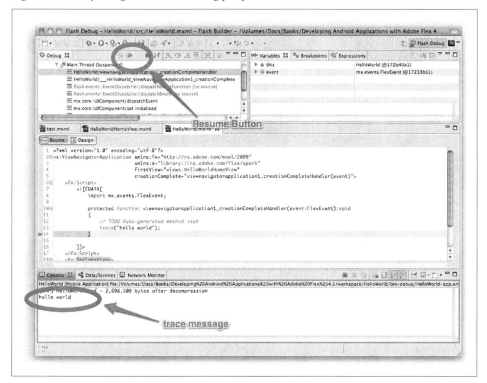

Figure 1-15. The Hello World application paused on line 14

CHAPTER 2

Application Layouts

When creating a Flex Mobile project, you have three choices for your layout. They are *Blank Application*, *View-Based Application*, and *Tabbed Application* (shown in Figure 2-1). The selection you make when choosing a layout will determine which files Flash Builder 4.5 will autogenerate. The View-Based and Tabbed Application types come with built-in navigation frameworks. Let's explore each of these.

Blank Application

The Blank Application layout is best used when you are planning to build your own custom navigation. Choosing this option when creating a new Flex Mobile application within Flash Builder 4.5 will create only the main application file, as shown in the code below:

```
<?xml version="1.0" encoding="utf-8"?>
<s:Application xmlns:fx="http://ns.adobe.com/mxml/2009"
               xmlns:s="library://ns.adobe.com/flex/spark">
    <fx:Declarations>
        <!-- Place non-visual elements (e.g., services, value objects) here -->
    </fx:Declarations>
</s:Application>
```

In the next code example, I have added a simple Label. You can see the results in Figure 2-2:

```
<?xml version="1.0" encoding="utf-8"?>
<s:Application xmlns:fx="http://ns.adobe.com/mxml/2009"
               xmlns:s="library://ns.adobe.com/flex/spark">
    <fx:Declarations>
        <!-- Place non-visual elements (e.g., services, value objects) here -->
    </fx:Declarations>
    <s:Label text="Blank" fontSize="36"
             horizontalCenter="0" verticalCenter="0"/>
</s:Application>
```

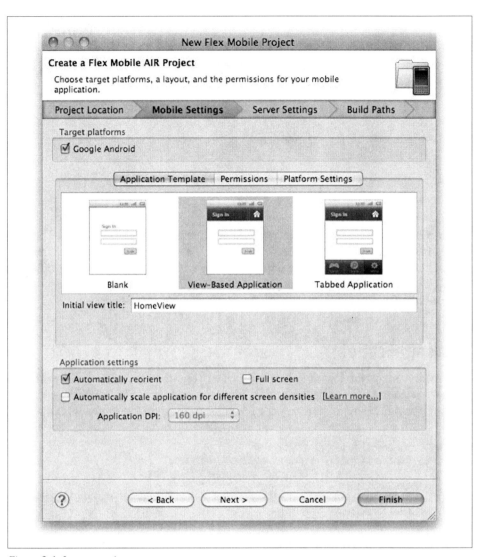

Figure 2-1. Layout options

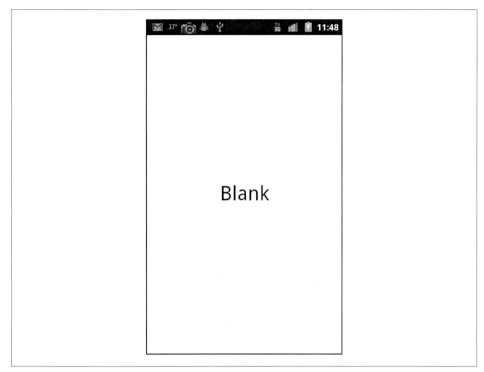

Figure 2-2. A Blank Application

View-Based Application

The View-Based Application adds the concept of a navigator, which is a built-in navigation framework specifically built for use within mobile applications. The navigator will manage the screens within your application. Creating a new View-Based Application within Flash Builder 4.5 will result in the generation of two files. These files are the main application file, as well as the default view that will be shown within your application. Unlike the Blank Application, where the main application file was created with the `<s:Application>` as the parent, a View-Based Application uses the new `<s:View NavigatorApplication>` as its parent, as shown below:

```
<?xml version="1.0" encoding="utf-8"?>
<s:ViewNavigatorApplication xmlns:fx="http://ns.adobe.com/mxml/2009"
                            xmlns:s="library://ns.adobe.com/flex/spark"
                            firstView="views.ViewBasedHomeView">
    <fx:Declarations>
        <!-- Place non-visual elements (e.g., services, value objects) here -->
    </fx:Declarations>
</s:ViewNavigatorApplication>
```

The second file that is created is the default view, which is automatically placed in a package named `views`. In this case, it was named `ViewBasedHomeView`, and was automatically set as the `firstView` property of `ViewNavigatorApplication`. The autogenerated code for this file is shown below:

```
<?xml version="1.0" encoding="utf-8"?>
<s:View xmlns:fx="http://ns.adobe.com/mxml/2009"
        xmlns:s="library://ns.adobe.com/flex/spark" title="HomeView">
    <fx:Declarations>
        <!-- Place non-visual elements (e.g., services, value objects) here -->
    </fx:Declarations>
</s:View>
```

Figure 2-3 shows the View-Based Application after adding a `Label` to `ViewBasedHome View`. As you can see, the navigation framework automatically provides a header and places the title of the current view in that header.

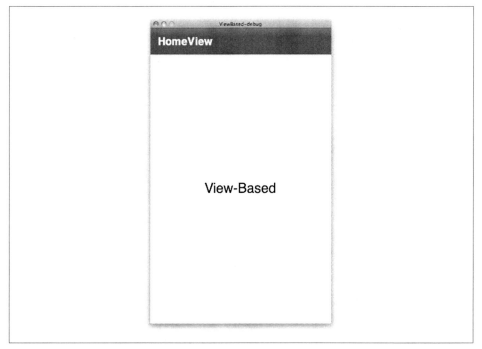

Figure 2-3. A View-Based Application

Now let's explore the navigator a bit. I have created a second view for my application named `SecondView`. I updated `ViewBasedHomeView` to have a `Button`, and also added a `Button` to the `SecondView` shown below. As you can see, each view contains a `Button` with a similar `clickHandler`. The `clickHandler` simply calls the `pushView` function on the navigator and passes in the view that you wish to have the user navigate to. Home-View will navigate to Second View, and Second View will navigate to HomeView.

Between each view, a transition is automatically played and the title of the view is reflected in the navigation bar. This can be seen in Figures 2-4 and 2-5:

```
<?xml version="1.0" encoding="utf-8"?>
<s:View xmlns:fx="http://ns.adobe.com/mxml/2009"
        xmlns:s="library://ns.adobe.com/flex/spark" title="HomeView">

    <fx:Script>
        <![CDATA[
            protectedfunction button1_clickHandler(event:MouseEvent):void
            {
                navigator.pushView(views.SecondView);
            }
        ]]>
    </fx:Script>

    <fx:Declarations>
        <!-- Place non-visual elements (e.g., services, value objects) here -->
    </fx:Declarations>

    <s:Button label="Go To Second View"
            horizontalCenter="0" verticalCenter="0"
              click="button1_clickHandler(event)"/>
</s:View>

<?xml version="1.0" encoding="utf-8"?>
<s:View xmlns:fx="http://ns.adobe.com/mxml/2009"
        xmlns:s="library://ns.adobe.com/flex/spark" title="SecondView">

    <fx:Script>
        <![CDATA[
            protectedfunction button1_clickHandler(event:MouseEvent):void
            {
                navigator.pushView(views.ViewBasedHomeView);
            }
        ]]>
    </fx:Script>

    <fx:Declarations>
        <!-- Place non-visual elements (e.g., services, value objects) here -->
    </fx:Declarations>

    <s:Button label="Go To Home View"
            horizontalCenter="0" verticalCenter="0"
              click="button1_clickHandler(event)"/>
</s:View>
```

Figure 2-4. The HomeView screen

Figure 2-5. The Second View screen

The navigator has additional methods for moving between views within your application. They are as follows:

`navigator.popAll()`

> Removes all of the views from the navigator stack. This method changes the display to a blank screen.

`navigator.popToFirstView()`

> Removes all views except the bottom view from the navigation stack. The bottom view is the one that was first pushed onto the stack.

`navigator.popView()`

> Pops the current view off the navigation stack. The current view is represented by the top view on the stack. The previous view on the stack becomes the current view.

`navigator.pushView()`

> Pushes a new view onto the top of the navigation stack. The view pushed onto the stack becomes the current view.

Each of the methods described above allow for a transition to be passed in. By default, they will use a Wipe transition. All pop actions will wipe from left to right, while a push action will wipe from right to left.

Another important item to note on `navigator.pushView()` is the ability to pass an object into the method call. I have updated the sample below to demonstrate how to use this within your applications.

The `ViewBasedHomeView` shown below now includes a piece of `String` data ("`Hello from Home View`") within the `pushView()` method. `SecondView` has also been updated to include a new `Label`, which is bound to the data object. This data object is what will hold the value of the object passed in through the `pushView()` method. Figure 2-6 shows how `SecondView` is created with the `Label` showing our new message:

```
<?xml version="1.0" encoding="utf-8"?>
<s:View xmlns:fx="http://ns.adobe.com/mxml/2009"
        xmlns:s="library://ns.adobe.com/flex/spark" title="HomeView">

    <fx:Script>
        <![CDATA[
            protectedfunction button1_clickHandler(event:MouseEvent):void
            {
                navigator.pushView(views.SecondView, "Hello from Home View");
            }
        ]]>
    </fx:Script>

    <fx:Declarations>
        <!-- Place non-visual elements (e.g., services, value objects) here -->
    </fx:Declarations>
    <s:Button label="Go To Second View"
              horizontalCenter="0" verticalCenter="0"
              click="button1_clickHandler(event)"/>
</s:View>
```

```
<?xml version="1.0" encoding="utf-8"?>
<s:View xmlns:fx="http://ns.adobe.com/mxml/2009"
        xmlns:s="library://ns.adobe.com/flex/spark" title="SecondView">

    <fx:Script>
        <![CDATA[
            protectedfunction button1_clickHandler(event:MouseEvent):void
            {
                navigator.pushView(views.ViewBasedHomeView);
            }
        ]]>
    </fx:Script>

    <fx:Declarations>
        <!-- Place non-visual elements (e.g., services, value objects) here -->
    </fx:Declarations>
    <s:Label text="{data}" horizontalCenter="0" top="30"/>
    <s:Button label="Go To Home View"
              horizontalCenter="0" verticalCenter="0"
              click="button1_clickHandler(event)"/>
</s:View>
```

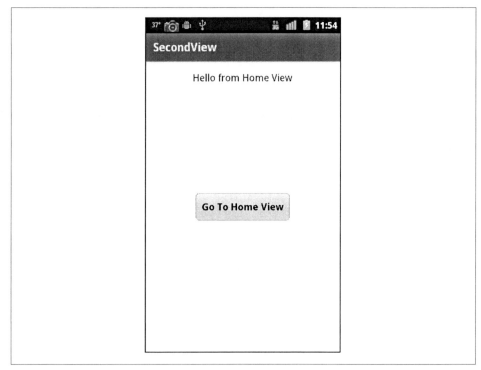

Figure 2-6. pushView() with data passed through

The navigation bar at the top of a View-Based Application allows you to set specific elements. These are navigationContent and actionContent. By setting these elements, your application can include a common navigation throughout. Here is an example of the View-Based Application's main file updated with these new elements. You will notice that navigationContent, actionContent, and the Spark components are defined in MXML. Within each, I have included a Button. Each Button has a clickHandler that includes a call to one of the navigator methods. The Button labeled "Home" has a click Handler that includes a call to the popToFirstView() method, which will always send the user back to the view defined in the firstView property of the ViewNavigation Application. The Button labeled "Back" has a clickHandler that includes a call to the popView() method, which will always send the user to the previous view in the stack.

 When using popView(), you will need to make sure your application is aware of where it is in the stack, as a call to popView() when the user is already on the firstView will send the user to a blank screen.

Figure 2-7 shows the application, which now includes the new navigation elements within the navigation bar:

```
<?xml version="1.0" encoding="utf-8"?>
<s:ViewNavigatorApplication xmlns:fx="http://ns.adobe.com/mxml/2009"
                            xmlns:s="library://ns.adobe.com/flex/spark"
                            firstView="views.ViewBasedHomeView">

    <fx:Script>
        <![CDATA[
            protectedfunction homeButton_clickHandler(event:MouseEvent):void
            {
                navigator.popToFirstView();
            }

            protectedfunction backButton_clickHandler(event:MouseEvent):void
            {
                navigator.popView();
            }

        ]]>
    </fx:Script>

    <fx:Declarations>
        <!-- Place non-visual elements (e.g., services, value objects) here -->
    </fx:Declarations>

    <s:navigationContent>

        <s:Button id="homeButton" click="homeButton_clickHandler(event)"
                  label="Home"/>

    </s:navigationContent>
```

```
    <s:actionContent>
        <s:Button id="backButton" click="backButton_clickHandler(event)"
                    label="Back"/>
    </s:actionContent>
</s:ViewNavigatorApplication>
```

 Although this example utilizes a Button component to demonstrate view navigation, the best practice when developing Android applications would be for your application to rely on the device's native back button navigation.

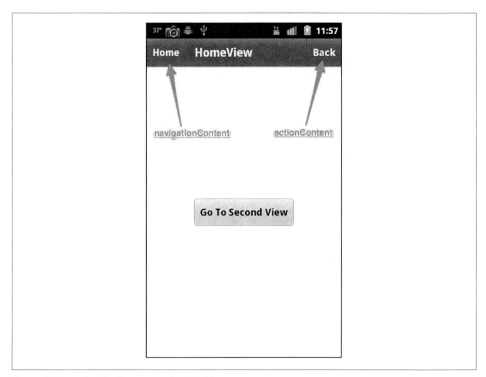

Figure 2-7. navigationContent and actionContent

View Life Cycle

The View class includes some new life cycle events specifically added for mobile applications. These events are important for application memory conservation:

- FlexEvent.VIEW_ACTIVATE is dispatched when the view has been activated:

    ```
    viewActivate="view1_viewActivateHandler(event)"
    ```

- `FlexEvent.VIEW_DEACTIVATE` is dispatched when the view has been deactivated:

  ```
  viewDeactivate="view1_viewDeactivateHandler(event)"
  ```

- `FlexEvent.REMOVING` is dispatched right before `FlexEvent.VIEW_DEACTIVATE`, when the view is about to be deactivated. Calling `preventDefault()` will cancel the screen change.

Although this life cycle is great for keeping the application's memory usage minimal, the default behavior to deactivate a view also destroys any data associated with that view. To preserve data so that it will be available if the user returns to that view, you can save the data to the `View.data` property.

If you would like to prevent a view from ever being deactivated, you can set the `destruc tionPolicy` attribute of the view (which normally defaults to `auto`) to `never`:

```
destructionPolicy="never"
```

Tabbed Application

The final option for application type is the Tabbed Application. Selecting Tabbed Application (see Figure 2-1) when creating a new Flex Mobile project will prompt Flash Builder to provide some additional functionality. As you can see within Figure 2-8, choosing Tabbed Application allows you to define your tabs right within the New Flex Mobile Project interface. In this example, I have added "My Application" and "My Preferences" tabs. After clicking Finish, Flash Builder will create my new Tabbed Application, as well as views for the tabs I defined. The code example below shows the contents of my main application file, named *Tabbed.mxml*. It is important to note that each of the views I defined (My Application and My Preferences) are included as `View Navigator` objects. This means that they will have their own navigator objects and can include their own independent navigation, just as within the View-Based Application we previously discussed. Figure 2-9 shows the running Tabbed Application. Figure 2-10 shows the View-Based Application views we previously created, within the *My Application* tab of the Tabbed Application:

```
<?xml version="1.0" encoding="utf-8"?>
<s:TabbedViewNavigatorApplication xmlns:fx="http://ns.adobe.com/mxml/2009"
                                  xmlns:s="library://ns.adobe.com/flex/spark">
    <s:ViewNavigator label="My Application" width="100%" height="100%"
                                  firstView="views._MyApplicationView"/>
    <s:ViewNavigator label="My Preferences" width="100%" height="100%"
                                  firstView="views._MyPreferencesView"/>
    <fx:Declarations>
        <!-- Place non-visual elements (e.g., services, value objects) here -->
    </fx:Declarations>
</s:TabbedViewNavigatorApplication>
```

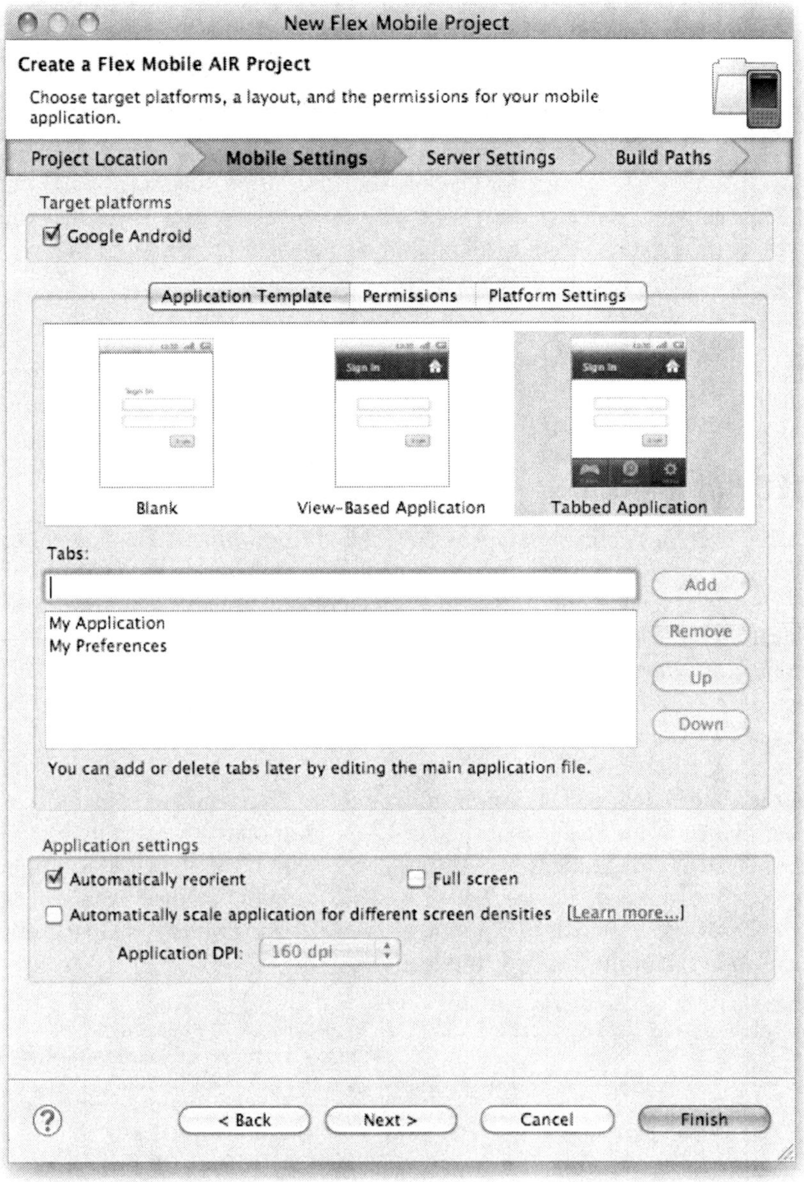

Figure 2-8. Create a new Tabbed Application

Figure 2-9. A Tabbed Application

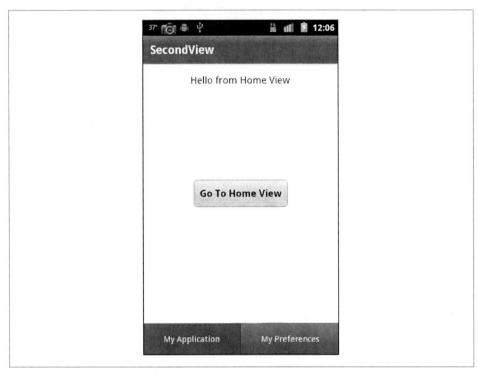

Figure 2-10. A Tabbed Application with navigators

CHAPTER 3

Permissions and Configuration Settings

When creating an Android application, it is necessary to select the permissions that your application will require to operate. As noted in "Create a Flex Mobile Project" in Chapter 1, it is important that you only select the permissions that your application needs to operate, because the application permissions requested will be used to filter which devices can install your application from the Android Market. There are also several other configuration settings, unique to Android applications, that will be covered in this chapter.

Permissions

The AIR 2.6 release includes the permission options outlined below, which can be selected within the new Flex Mobile project interface of Flash Builder 4.5. This is shown in Figure 3-1. Figure 3-2 shows the warning the user will see when installing an application with permission requests. The permissions are:

INTERNET
> Allows applications to open sockets and embed HTML content.

WRITE_EXTERNAL_STORAGE
> Allows an application to write to external storage.

READ_PHONE_STATE
> Allows the AIR Runtime to mute audio from application, in case of incoming call.

ACCESS_FINE_LOCATION
> Allows an application to access GPS location.

DISABLE_KEYGUARD, WAKE_LOCK
> Allows applications to access screen dimming provision.

CAMERA
> Allows applications to access device camera.

RECORD_AUDIO
Allows applications to access device microphone.

ACCESS_NETWORK_STATE, ACCESS_WIFI_STATE
Allows applications to access information about network interfaces associated with the device.

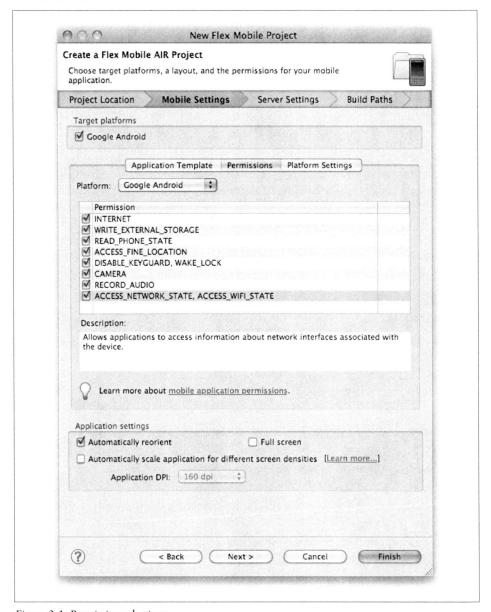

Figure 3-1. Permission selections

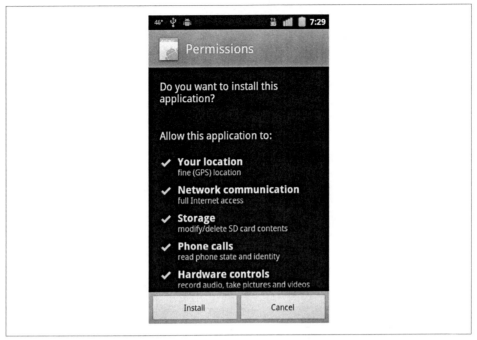

Figure 3-2. Installer permission warnings

These permissions are also editable within the application's XML configuration file.

 Manually editing the configurations within the application's XML configuration file is the only way to make permission changes once you have created the mobile project.

Here is a sample of what that looks like:

```
<android>
    <manifestAdditions><![CDATA[
        <manifest installLocation="auto">
        <!--See the Adobe AIR documentation for more information about setting
            Google Android permissions-->
        <!--Removing the permission android.permission.INTERNET will have the
            side effect of preventing you from debugging your application
            on your device-->
        <uses-permission name="android.permission.INTERNET"/>
        <!--<uses-permission name="android.permission.WRITE_EXTERNAL_STORAGE"/>-->
        <!--<uses-permission name="android.permission.READ_PHONE_STATE"/>-->
        <!--<uses-permission name="android.permission.ACCESS_FINE_LOCATION"/>-->
        <!--The DISABLE_KEYGUARD and WAKE_LOCK permissions should be toggled
            together in order to access AIR's SystemIdleMode APIs-->
        <!--<uses-permission name="android.permission.DISABLE_KEYGUARD"/>-->
        <!--<uses-permission name="android.permission.WAKE_LOCK"/>-->
        <!--<uses-permission name="android.permission.CAMERA"/>-->
```

```
            <!--<uses-permission name="android.permission.RECORD_AUDIO"/>-->
            <!--The ACCESS_NETWORK_STATE and ACCESS_WIFI_STATE permissions should be
                toggled together in order to use AIR's NetworkInfo APIs-->
            <!--<uses-permission name="android.permission.ACCESS_NETWORK_STATE"/>-->
            <!--<uses-permission name="android.permission.ACCESS_WIFI_STATE"/>-->
    </manifest>

    ]]></manifestAdditions>
</android>
```

Other Configuration Settings

When creating a new Flex Mobile application, there are a few additional settings that you can choose to configure. These include Automatically reorient; Full screen; and Automatically scale application for different screen densities. Figure 3-3 shows these options.

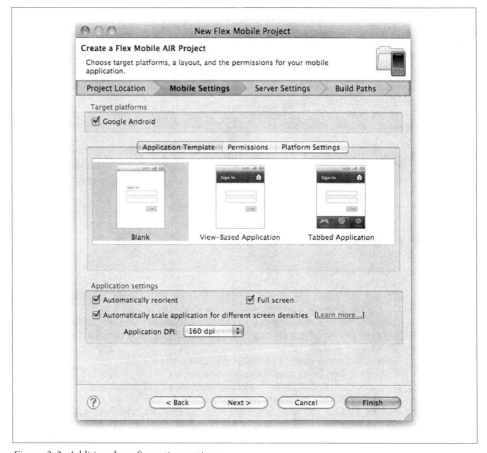

Figure 3-3. Additional configuration settings

Automatically Reorient

This option is set to true automatically, unless you uncheck the box during your project creation. Setting this to true will allow the device to use its accelerometer to automatically switch between portrait and landscape.

This property can be edited at any time within the application's configuration file. This setting can also be changed programmatically while the application is running (see Chapter 5 for more information on this):

```
<autoOrients>false</autoOrients>
```

Full Screen

Checking this box during your project creation will force your application to launch in full screen mode. By default, this is set to false.

This property can be edited at any time within the application's XML configuration file. This setting can also be changed programmatically while the application is running (see Chapter 5 for more information on this):

```
<fullScreen>false</fullScreen>
```

Automatically Scale Application for Different Screen Densities

Checking this box will allow your application to automatically scale for different screen densities. It will also allow you to set the default `applicationDPI` which will be written to the main application file. The options for this value are 160, 240, or 320:

```
<s:Application xmlns:fx="http://ns.adobe.com/mxml/2009"
               xmlns:s="library://ns.adobe.com/flex/spark"
               applicationDPI="320">
```

Aspect Ratio

You have the option to force an application to only run in portrait or landscape mode. You can accomplish this by uncommenting the `<aspectRatio>` node within the application's XML configuration file, and setting its value to either `landscape` or `portrait`. This setting can also be changed programmatically while the application is running (see Chapter 5 for more information on this):

```
<aspectRatio>landscape</aspectRatio>
```

CHAPTER 4

Exploring the APIs

Now that you know how to create a new application with various layout options and how to request application permissions, it is time to explore the ways in which your application can interact with the Android operating system. The AIR 2.6 release includes access to many Android features. These include the accelerometer, the GPS unit, the camera, the camera roll, the file system and the multitouch screen.

 Up until this point, I have compiled the sample applications to the ADL simulator. However, to demonstrate the API integrations, it is necessary to run the applications on an Android device. The screenshots in this section are from an HTC NexusOne phone. Instructions on how to run an application on an Android device are included in Chapter 1.

Accelerometer

The accelerometer is a device that measures the speed or g-forces created when a device accelerates across multiple planes. The faster the device is moved through space, the higher the readings will be across the x, y, and z axes.

Let's review the code below. First, you will notice that there is a private variable named accelerometer declared, of type flash.sensors.Accelerometer. Within applicationCom plete of the application, an event handler function is called, which first checks to see if the device has an accelerometer by reading the static property of the Accelerometer class. If this property returns as true, a new instance of Accelerometer is created and an event listener of type AccelerometerEvent.UPDATE is added to handle updates. Upon update, the accelerometer information is read from the event and written to a Text Area within the handleUpdate function. The results can be seen within Figure 4-1:

```
<?xml version="1.0" encoding="utf-8"?>
<s:Application xmlns:fx="http://ns.adobe.com/mxml/2009"
               xmlns:s="library://ns.adobe.com/flex/spark"
               applicationComplete="application1_applicationCompleteHandler(event)">
    <fx:Script>
        <![CDATA[
            import flash.sensors.Accelerometer;

            import mx.events.FlexEvent;

            privatevar accelerometer:Accelerometer;

            protectedfunction application1_applicationCompleteHandler
                (event:FlexEvent):void {
                  if(Accelerometer.isSupported==true){
                      accelerometer = new Accelerometer();
                      accelerometer.addEventListener(AccelerometerEvent.
                          UPDATE,handleUpdate);
                  } else {
                      status.text = "Accelerometer not supported";
                  }

            }

            privatefunction handleUpdate(event:AccelerometerEvent):void {
                  info.text = "Updated: " + new Date().toTimeString() + "\n\n"
                  + "acceleration X: "+ event.accelerationX + "\n"
                  + "acceleration Y: " + event.accelerationY + "\n"
                  + "acceleration Z: " + event.accelerationZ;
            }

        ]]>
    </fx:Script>

    <fx:Declarations>
        <!-- Place non-visual elements (e.g., services, value objects) here -->
    </fx:Declarations>
    <s:Label id="status" text="Shake your phone a bit" top="10" width="100%"
        textAlign="center"/>
    <s:TextArea id="info" width="100%" height="200" top="40" editable="false"/>
</s:Application>
```

Figure 4-1. Accelerometer information

GPS

GPS stands for Global Positioning System. GPS is a space-based satellite navigation system, which provides reliable location information to your handheld device.

If your application requires the use of the device's GPS, you will need to select the ACCESS_FINE_LOCATION permission when you are creating your project. See Chapter 3 for help with permissions.

Let's review the code below. First, you will notice that there is a private variable named `geoLocation` declared, of type `flash.sensors.GeoLocation`. Within `application Complete` of the application, an event handler function is called, which first checks to see if the device has an available GPS unit by reading the static property of the `GeoLocation` class. If this property returns as true, a new instance of `GeoLocation` is created; the data refresh interval is set to 500 milliseconds (.5 seconds) within the `setRequestedUpdateInterval` method; and an event listener of type `GeoLocation Event.UPDATE` is added to handle updates. Upon update, the GPS information is read from the event and written to a `TextArea` within the `handleUpdate` function.

There is also some math being done to convert the speed property into miles per hour and kilometers per hour.

The results can be seen within Figure 4-2:

```
<?xml version="1.0" encoding="utf-8"?>
<s:Application xmlns:fx="http://ns.adobe.com/mxml/2009"
               xmlns:s="library://ns.adobe.com/flex/spark"
               applicationComplete="application1_applicationCompleteHandler(event)">
    <fx:Script>
        <![CDATA[
            import mx.events.FlexEvent;

            import flash.sensors.Geolocation;

            private var geoLocation:Geolocation;

            protected function application1_applicationCompleteHandler
                (event:FlexEvent):void {
                  if(Geolocation.isSupported==true){
                      geoLocation = new Geolocation();
                      geoLocation.setRequestedUpdateInterval(500);
                      geoLocation.addEventListener(GeolocationEvent.UPDATE,
                          handleLocationRequest);
                  } else {
                      status.text = "Geolocation feature not supported";
                  }
            }

            private function handleLocationRequest(event:GeolocationEvent):void {
                var mph:Number = event.speed*2.23693629;
                var kph:Number = event.speed*3.6;
                info.text = "Updated: " + new Date().toTimeString() + "\n\n"
                    + "latitude: " + event.latitude.toString() + "\n"
                    + "longitude: " + event.longitude.toString() + "\n"
                    + "altitude: " + event.altitude.toString()  + "\n"
                    + "speed: " + event.speed.toString()  + "\n"
                    + "speed: " + mph.toString()  + " MPH \n"
                    + "speed: " + kph.toString()  + " KPH \n"
                    + "heading: " + event.heading.toString()  + "\n"
                    + "horizontal accuracy: "
                    + event.horizontalAccuracy.toString()  + "\n"
                    + "vertical accuracy: "
                    + event.verticalAccuracy.toString();
            }
        ]]>
    </fx:Script>
    <fx:Declarations>
        <!-- Place non-visual elements (e.g., services, value objects) here -->
    </fx:Declarations>
```

```
    <s:Label id="status" text="Geolocation Info" top="10" width="100%"
        textAlign="center"/>
    <s:TextArea id="info" width="100%" top="40" editable="false"/>
</s:Application>
```

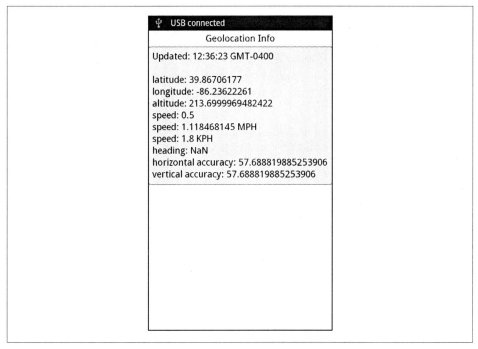

Figure 4-2. GPS information

Camera UI

A camera is almost ubiquitous on handheld Android devices. In fact, many new Android devices now include both front- and rear-facing cameras.

If your application requires the use of the device's camera, you will need to select the
CAMERA permission when you are creating your project (see Chapter 3 for help with
permissions). The Camera UI tools will allow your application to use the native Camera
interface within the Android device.

Let's review the code below. First, you will notice there is a private variable named
camera declared, of type flash.media.CameraUI. Within applicationComplete of the application, an event handler function is called, which first checks to see if the device has
an available camera by reading the static property of the CameraUI class. If this property
returns as true, a new instance of CameraUI is created and event listeners of type Media
Event.COMPLETE and ErrorEvent.COMPLETE are added to handle a successfully captured
image as well as any errors that may occur.

A `Button` with an event listener on the `click` event is used to allow the application user to launch the `CameraUI`. When the user clicks the TAKE A PICTURE button, the `captureImage` method is called, which then opens the camera by calling the `launch` method and passing in the `MediaType.IMAGE` static property. At this point, the user is redirected from your application to the native camera. Once the user takes a picture and clicks OK, he is directed back to your application, the `MediaEvent.COMPLETE` event is triggered, and the `onComplete` method is called. Within the `onComplete` method, the `event.data` property is cast to a `flash.Media.MediaPromise` object. The `mediaPromise.file.url` property is then used to populate `Label` and `Image` components that display the path to the image and the actual image to the user.

 Utilizing `CameraUI` within your application is different than the raw camera access provided by Adobe AIR on the desktop. Raw camera access is also available within AIR on Android and works in the same way as the desktop version.

Figure 4-3 shows the application, Figure 4-4 shows the native camera user interface, and Figure 4-5 shows the application after a picture was taken and the user clicked OK to return to the application:

```
<?xml version="1.0" encoding="utf-8"?>
<s:Application xmlns:fx="http://ns.adobe.com/mxml/2009"
               xmlns:s="library://ns.adobe.com/flex/spark"
               applicationComplete="application1_applicationCompleteHandler(event)">
    <fx:Script>
        <![CDATA[
            import mx.events.FlexEvent;

            privatevar camera:CameraUI;

            protectedfunction application1_applicationCompleteHandler
                (event:FlexEvent):void {
                if (CameraUI.isSupported){
                    camera = new CameraUI();
                    camera.addEventListener(MediaEvent.COMPLETE, onComplete);
                    camera.addEventListener(ErrorEvent.ERROR, onError);
                    status.text="CameraUI supported";
                } else {
                    status.text="CameraUI NOT supported";
                }
            }

            privatefunction captureImage(event:MouseEvent):void {
                camera.launch(MediaType.IMAGE);
            }

            privatefunction onError(event:ErrorEvent):void {
                trace("error has occurred");
            }
```

```
            privatefunction onComplete(event:MediaEvent):void {
                    var mediaPromise:MediaPromise = event.data;
                    status.text = mediaPromise.file.url;
                    image.source = mediaPromise.file.url;
            }

        ]]>
    </fx:Script>
    <fx:Declarations>
        <!-- Place non-visual elements (e.g., services, value objects) here -->
    </fx:Declarations>

    <s:Label id="status" text="Click Take a Picture button" top="10" width="100%"
        textAlign="center"/>

    <s:Button width="300" height="60" label="TAKE A PICTURE"
        click="captureImage(event)"
                horizontalCenter="0" enabled="{CameraUI.isSupported}"
                top="80"/>

    <s:Image id="image" width="230" height="350" horizontalCenter="0" top="170"/>
</s:Application>
```

Figure 4-3. The Camera UI Application

Figure 4-4. The native camera UI

Figure 4-5. Application after taking picture

Camera Roll

The Camera Roll provides access to the camera's gallery of images.

If your application requires the use of the device's camera roll, you will need to select the WRITE_EXTERNAL_STORAGE permission when you are creating your project. See Chapter 3 for help with permissions.

Let's review the code below. First, you will notice that there is a private variable named `cameraRoll` declared, of type `flash.media.CameraRoll`. Within `applicationComplete` of the application, an event handler function is called, which first checks to see if the device supports access to the image gallery by reading the static property of the `CameraRoll` class. If this property returns as true, a new instance of `CameraRoll` is created and event listeners of type `MediaEvent.COMPLETE` and `ErrorEvent.COMPLETE` are added to handle a successfully captured image (as well as any errors that may occur).

A `Button` with an event listener on the `click` event is used to allow the user to browse the image gallery. When the user clicks the BROWSEGALLERY button, the `browse Gallery` method is called, which then opens the device's image gallery. At this point, the user is redirected from your application to the native gallery application. Once the user selects an image from the gallery, she is directed back to your application, the `MediaEvent.COMPLETE` event is triggered, and the `mediaSelected` method is called. Within the `mediaSelected` method, the `event.data` property is cast to a `flash.Media.MediaPro mise` object. The `mediaPromise.file.url` property is then used to populate `Label` and `Image` components that display the path to the image and the actual image to the user. Figure 4-6 shows the application and Figure 4-7 shows the application after a picture was selected from the gallery and the user has returned to the application:

```
<?xml version="1.0" encoding="utf-8"?>
<s:Application xmlns:fx="http://ns.adobe.com/mxml/2009"
               xmlns:s="library://ns.adobe.com/flex/spark"
               applicationComplete="application1_applicationCompleteHandler(event)">
    <fx:Script>
        <![CDATA[
            import mx.events.FlexEvent;

            privatevar cameraRoll:CameraRoll;

            protectedfunction application1_applicationCompleteHandler
                (event:FlexEvent):void {
                    if(CameraRoll.supportsBrowseForImage){
                        cameraRoll = new CameraRoll();
                        cameraRoll.addEventListener(MediaEvent.SELECT,
                            mediaSelected);
                        cameraRoll.addEventListener(ErrorEvent.ERROR, onError);
                    } else{
                        status.text="CameraRoll NOT supported";
                    }
                }
```

```
            privatefunction browseGallery(event:MouseEvent):void {
                    cameraRoll.browseForImage();
            }

            privatefunction onError(event:ErrorEvent):void {
                    trace("error has occurred");
            }

            privatefunction mediaSelected(event:MediaEvent):void{
                    var mediaPromise:MediaPromise = event.data;
                    status.text = mediaPromise.file.url;
                    image.source = mediaPromise.file.url;
            }
        ]]>
    </fx:Script>
    <fx:Declarations>
        <!-- Place non-visual elements (e.g., services, value objects) here -->
    </fx:Declarations>

    <s:Label id="status" text="Click Browse Gallery to select image" top="10"
        width="100%" textAlign="center"/>

    <s:Button width="300" height="60" label="BROWSE GALLERY"
        click="browseGallery(event)"
                enabled="{CameraRoll.supportsBrowseForImage}"
                top="80" horizontalCenter="0"/>

    <s:Image id="image" width="230" height="350" top="170" horizontalCenter="0"/>
</s:Application>
```

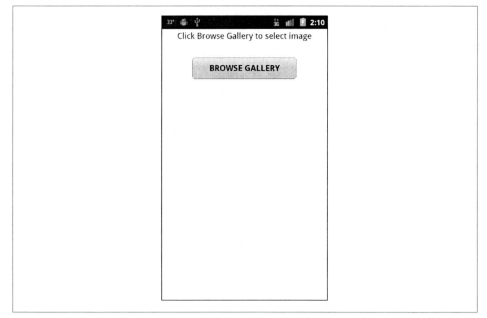

Figure 4-6. The Browse Gallery application

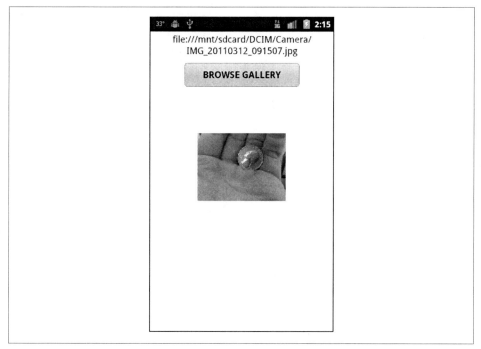

Figure 4-7. The Browse Gallery application with a picture selected

Microphone

If your application requires the use of the device's microphone, you will need to select the RECORD_AUDIO permission when you are creating your project. See Chapter 3 for help with permissions.

Let's review the code below. First, you will notice that there is a private variable named microphone declared, of type `flash.media.Microphone`. Within `applicationComplete` of the application, an event handler function is called, which first checks to see if the device supports access to the microphone by reading the static property of the `Microphone` class. If this property returns as true, an instance of the `Microphone` is retrieved and set to the microphone variable, the `rate` is set to `44`, and the `setUseEchoSuppression` method is used to set the echo suppression to true. There are also variables of type `ByteArray` and `Sound` declared within this application (instances of these variables will be created when the application runs).

There are three button components within the application to trigger the record, stop, and playback functionalities, respectively.

Clicking the record button will call the `record_clickHandler` function, which will create a new instance of the recording variable of type `ByteArray`. An event listener of type `SampleDataEvent.SAMPLE_DATA` is added to the microphone, which will call the `micData Handler` method when it receives data. Within the `micDataHandler` method, the data is written to the recording `ByteArray`.

Clicking the stop button will stop the recording by removing the `SampleDataEvent. SAMPLE_DATA` event listener.

Clicking the play button will call the `play_clickHandler` method, which first sets the position of the recording `ByteArray` to 0 so it is ready for playback. It then creates a new instance of the `Sound` class and sets it to the **sound** variable. It also adds an event listener of type `SampleDataEvent.SAMPLE_DATA` that will call the `playSound` method when it receives data. Finally the play method is called on the sound variable to start playback.

The `playSound` method loops through the recording `ByteArray` in memory and writes those bytes back to the data property of the `SampleDataEvent`, which then plays through the device's speaker.

To extend this sample, you would need to use some open source classes to convert the recording `ByteArray` to an *.mp3* or *.wav* file so that it can be saved to disk. See the application in Figure 4-8:

```
<?xml version="1.0" encoding="utf-8"?>
<s:Application xmlns:fx="http://ns.adobe.com/mxml/2009"
              xmlns:s="library://ns.adobe.com/flex/spark"
              applicationComplete="application1_applicationCompleteHandler(event)">
    <fx:Script>
        <![CDATA[
            import mx.events.FlexEvent;

            privatevar microphone:Microphone;
            privatevar recording:ByteArray;
            privatevar sound:Sound;

            protectedfunction application1_applicationCompleteHandler
                (event:FlexEvent):void
            {
                if(Microphone.isSupported){
                    microphone = Microphone.getMicrophone();
                    microphone.rate = 44;
                    microphone.setUseEchoSuppression(true);
                } else {
                    status.text="Microphone NOT supported";
                }
            }

            privatefunction micDataHandler(event:SampleDataEvent):void{
                recording.writeBytes(event.data);
            }

            protectedfunction record_clickHandler(event:MouseEvent):void
            {
```

```
            recording = new ByteArray();
            microphone.addEventListener(SampleDataEvent.SAMPLE_DATA,
                micDataHandler);
        }

        protectedfunction stop_clickHandler(event:MouseEvent):void
        {
            microphone.removeEventListener(SampleDataEvent.SAMPLE_DATA,
                micDataHandler);
        }

        protectedfunction play_clickHandler(event:MouseEvent):void
        {
            recording.position = 0;
            sound = new Sound();
            sound.addEventListener(SampleDataEvent.SAMPLE_DATA, playSound);
            sound.play();
        }

        privatefunction playSound(event:SampleDataEvent):void
        {
            for (var i:int = 0; i < 8192 && recording.bytesAvailable > 0;
                i++){
                var sample:Number = recording.readFloat();
                event.data.writeFloat(sample);
                event.data.writeFloat(sample);
            }
        }

    ]]>
</fx:Script>
<fx:Declarations>
    <!-- Place non-visual elements (e.g., services, value objects) here -->
</fx:Declarations>

<s:Label id="status" text="Click Record to grab some audio,
    then Stop and Play it back"
        top="10" width="100%" textAlign="center"/>
<s:HGrouptop="80" horizontalCenter="0">
    <s:Button id="record" label="Record" click="record_clickHandler(event)" />
    <s:Button id="stop" label="Stop" click="stop_clickHandler(event)" />
    <s:Button id="play" label="Play" click="play_clickHandler(event)" />
</s:HGroup>
</s:Application>
```

Figure 4-8. The microphone application

Multitouch

One of the navigation methods unique to mobile devices is the ability to interact with an application via gestures on the device's touchscreen. Multitouch is defined as the ability to simultaneously register three or more touch points on the device. Within Adobe AIR 2.6, there are two event classes used to listen for multitouch events.

GestureEvent

The GestureEvent class is used to listen for a two-finger tap on the device. The event used to listen for this action is GESTURE_TWO_FINGER_TAP. This event will return the registration points for the x and y coordinates when a two-finger tap occurs for both stage positioning as well as object positioning.

Let's review the code below. Within applicationComplete of the application, an event handler function is called, which first sets the Multitouch.inputMode to Multitouch InputMode.GESTURE. Next, it checks to see if the device supports multitouch by reading the static property of the Multitouch class. If this property returns as true, an event listener is added to the stage to listen for GestureEvent.GESTURE_TWO_FINGER_TAP events. When this event occurs, the onGestureTwoFinderTap method is called., which will capture the localX and localY coordinates as well as the stageX and stageY coordinates. If you two-finger-tap on an empty portion of the stage, these values will be identical. If you two-finger-tap on an object on the stage, the localX and localY coordinates will be the values within the object, and the stageX and stageY will be relative to the stage itself. See Figure 4-9 for an example of a two-finger tap on the stage and Figure 4-10 for a two-finger tap on the Android image:

```
<?xml version="1.0" encoding="utf-8"?>
<s:Application xmlns:fx="http://ns.adobe.com/mxml/2009"
               xmlns:s="library://ns.adobe.com/flex/spark"
               applicationComplete="application1_applicationCompleteHandler(event)">
    <fx:Script>
        <![CDATA[
            import mx.events.FlexEvent;

            protectedfunction application1_applicationCompleteHandler
                (event:FlexEvent):void {
                Multitouch.inputMode = MultitouchInputMode.GESTURE;
                if(Multitouch.supportsGestureEvents){
                    stage.addEventListener(GestureEvent.GESTURE_TWO_FINGER_TAP,
                        onGestureTwoFingerTap);
                } else {
                    status.text="gestures not supported";
                }

            }
            privatefunction onGestureTwoFingerTap(event:GestureEvent):void {
                info.text = "event = " + event.type + "\n" +
                    "localX = " + event.localX + "\n" +
                    "localX = " + event.localY + "\n" +
                    "stageX = " + event.stageX + "\n" +
                    "stageY = " + event.stageY;
            }

        ]]>
    </fx:Script>
    <fx:Declarations>
        <!-- Place non-visual elements (e.g., services, value objects) here -->
    </fx:Declarations>
    <s:Label id="status" text="Do a 2 finger tap both on and off the object"
            top="10" width="100%" textAlign="center"/>
    <s:TextArea id="info" width="100%" top="40" editable="false"/>
    <s:Image width="384" height="384" bottom="10" horizontalCenter="0"
            source="@Embed('android_icon.png')"/>
</s:Application>
```

Figure 4-9. A two-finger tap on the stage

Figure 4-10. A two-finger tap on an image object

TransformGesture

There are multiple transform gesture events available within AIR 2.6. Each will capture a unique multitouch event. The example below demonstrates how to listen for GESTURE_PAN, GESTURE_ROTATE, GESTURE_SWIPE, and GESTURE_ZOOM events.

Let's review the code below. Within applicationComplete of the application, an event handler function is called, which first sets the Multitouch.inputMode to Multitouch InputMode.GESTURE. Next, it checks to see if the device supports multitouch by reading the static property of the Multitouch class. If this property returns as true, event listeners are added to the stage to listen for the TransformGestureEvent.GESTURE_PAN, Transform GestureEvent.GESTURE_ROTATE, TransformGestureEvent.GESTURE_SWIPE, and Transform GestureEvent.GESTURE_ZOOM events.

When a user grabs an object with two fingers and drags it, the TransformGesture Event.GESTURE_PAN event is triggered and the onGesturePan method is called. Within the onGesturePan method, the offsetX and offsetY values of this event are written to the text property of the TextArea component. Adding the event's offsetX and offsetY values sets the object's x and y to move the object across the stage. The results can be seen in Figure 4-11.

Figure 4-11. The GESTURE_PAN event

When a user grabs an object with two fingers and rotates it, the `TransformGesture` `Event.GESTURE_ROTATE` event is triggered and the `onGestureRotate` method is called. Within the `onGestureRotate` method, the rotation value of this event is written to the `text` property of the *TextArea* component. To allow the object to rotate around its center, the object's `transformAround` method is called and the event's rotation value is added to the object's `rotationZ` value. The results can be seen in Figure 4-12.

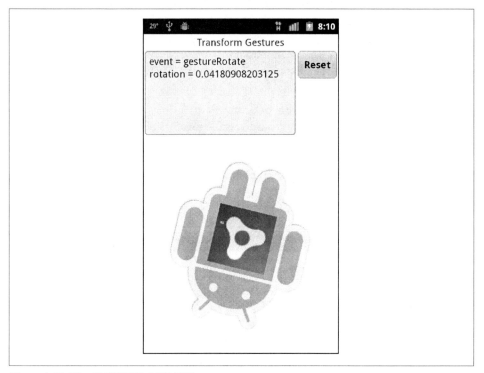

Figure 4-12. The GESTURE_ROTATE event

When a user swipes across an object with one finger in any direction, the `Transform` `GestureEvent.GESTURE_SWIPE` event is triggered and the `onGestureSwipe` method is called. Within the `onGestureSwipe` method, the values of the event's `offsetX` and `offsetY` are evaluated to determine the direction in which the user swiped across the object. This direction is then written to the `text` property of the `TextArea` component. The results can be seen in Figure 4-13.

Figure 4-13. The GESTURE_SWIPE event

When a user performs a "pinch and zoom" action with two fingers on an object, the
TransformGestureEvent.GESTURE_ZOOM event is triggered and the onGestureZoom method
is called. Within the onGestureZoom method, the values of the event's scaleX and
scaleY are written to the text property of the TextArea component. The scaleX value
is then used as a multiplier on the object's scaleX and scaleY property to increase or
decrease the size of the object as the user pinches or expands two fingers on the object.
The results can be seen in Figure 4-14:

```
<?xml version="1.0" encoding="utf-8"?>
<s:Application xmlns:fx="http://ns.adobe.com/mxml/2009"
               xmlns:s="library://ns.adobe.com/flex/spark"
               applicationComplete="application1_applicationCompleteHandler(event)">
    <fx:Script>
        <![CDATA[
            import mx.events.FlexEvent;

            protectedfunction application1_applicationCompleteHandler
                (event:FlexEvent):void {
                Multitouch.inputMode = MultitouchInputMode.GESTURE;
                if(Multitouch.supportsGestureEvents){
                    image.addEventListener(TransformGestureEvent.GESTURE_PAN,
                    onGesturePan);
```

```
                    image.addEventListener(TransformGestureEvent.GESTURE_ROTATE,
                        onGestureRotate);
                    image.addEventListener(TransformGestureEvent.GESTURE_SWIPE,
                        onGestureSwipe);
                    image.addEventListener(TransformGestureEvent.GESTURE_ZOOM,
                        onGestureZoom);
            } else {
                status.text="gestures not supported";
            }
    }

    privatefunction onGesturePan(event:TransformGestureEvent):void{
            info.text = "event = " + event.type + "\n" +
            "offsetX = " + event.offsetX + "\n" +
            "offsetY = " + event.offsetY;
            image.x += event.offsetX;
            image.y += event.offsetY;
    }

    privatefunction onGestureRotate( event :
        TransformGestureEvent ) : void {
            info.text = "event = " + event.type + "\n" +
            "rotation = " + event.rotation;
            image.transformAround(new Vector3D(image.width/2,
                                                image.height/2, 0),
                                    null,
                                    new Vector3D(0,0,image.rotationZ
                                        + event.rotation));
    }

    privatefunction onGestureSwipe( event :
        TransformGestureEvent ) : void {
            var direction:String = "";
            if(event.offsetX == 1) direction = "right";
            if(event.offsetX == -1) direction = "left";
            if(event.offsetY == 1) direction = "down";
            if(event.offsetY == -1) direction = "up";
            info.text = "event = " + event.type + "\n" +
            "direction = " + direction;
    }

    privatefunction onGestureZoom( event :
        TransformGestureEvent ) : void {
            info.text = "event = " + event.type + "\n" +
            "scaleX = " + event.scaleX + "\n" +
            "scaleY = " + event.scaleY;
            image.scaleX = image.scaleY *= event.scaleX;
    }

    protectedfunction button1_clickHandler(event:MouseEvent):void
    {
            image.rotation = 0;
            image.scaleX = 1;
            image.scaleY = 1;
```

```
                image.x = 40;
                image.y = 260;
                info.text = "";
        }

    ]]>
</fx:Script>
<fx:Declarations>
        <!-- Place non-visual elements (e.g., services, value objects) here -->
</fx:Declarations>
<s:Label id="status" text="Transform Gestures" top="10" width="100%"
    textAlign="center"/>
<s:HGroup width="100%" top="40" left="5" right="5">
    <s:TextArea id="info" editable="false" width="100%" height="200"/>
    <s:Button label="Reset" click="button1_clickHandler(event)"/>
</s:HGroup>
<s:Image id="image" x="40" y="260" width="400" height="400"
            source="@Embed('android_icon.png')"/>
</s:Application>
```

Figure 4-14. The GESTURE_ZOOM event

Busy Indicator

A new component has been added to provide feedback to the users within your mobile application. While there is no cursor to show busy status as there is in desktop development, the BusyIndicator component was added specifically for this reason. Using this component is extremely simple.

Let's review the code below. There is a CheckBox with the label "Show Busy Indicator", which when checked, calls the checkbox1_clickHandler method. There is a Busy Indicator component with an id of indicator, set to visible (or false). Within the checkbox1_clickHandler method, the indicator's visible property is set to the value of the CheckBox. This simply shows or hides the BusyIndicator. Within the BusyIndicator, you can set the height, width, and symbolColor to suit the needs and style of your application. The results can be seen in Figure 4-15:

```
<?xml version="1.0" encoding="utf-8"?>
<s:Application xmlns:fx="http://ns.adobe.com/mxml/2009"
               xmlns:s="library://ns.adobe.com/flex/spark">

    <fx:Script>
        <![CDATA[
            protectedfunction checkbox1_clickHandler(event:MouseEvent):void
            {
                indicator.visible = event.target.selected;
            }
        ]]>
    </fx:Script>

    <fx:Declarations>
        <!-- Place non-visual elements (e.g., services, value objects) here -->
    </fx:Declarations>

    <s:CheckBox label="Show Busy Indicator"
                horizontalCenter="0"
                click="checkbox1_clickHandler(event)" top="10"/>
    <s:BusyIndicator id="indicator" height="300" width="300"
                     verticalCenter="0"
                     horizontalCenter="0"
                     visible="false"
                     symbolColor="black"/>

</s:Application>
```

Figure 4-15. The BusyIndicator component

CHAPTER 5

Working with the File System

AIR on Android provides access to the file system to read, write, and update files of all types. This functionality can be very useful not only for reading existing files, but also for storing files, media, data, and so on. This chapter will demonstrate how to read and write text files, browse the file system for media files, and create and write to an SQLite database.

This chapter has sample applications that require access to the file system, so you will need to select the WRITE_EXTERNAL_STORAGE permission when you are creating these projects. See Chapter 3 for help with permissions.

File System Access

Just as in the desktop version of Adobe AIR, AIR on Android gives you access to the file system. The usage is exactly the same.

Folder Aliases

To access the file system, you can navigate using several folder static alias properties of the File class.

Let's review the code below. On applicationComplete, the application1_application CompleteHandler method is called, and the static File properties are read and written to a String variable. This String variable is written to the text property of a TextArea component. Figure 5-1 shows the results. You will notice that many of the aliases return the same value, which is a path to the device's external storage card:

```
<?xml version="1.0" encoding="utf-8"?>
<s:Application xmlns:fx="http://ns.adobe.com/mxml/2009"
               xmlns:s="library://ns.adobe.com/flex/spark"
               applicationComplete="application1_applicationCompleteHandler(event)">
    <fx:Script>
        <![CDATA[
            import mx.events.FlexEvent;
```

```
                  protectedfunction application1_applicationCompleteHandler
                      (event:FlexEvent):void
                  {
                          var s:String = "";
                          s += "File.applicationDirectory : " +
                              File.applicationDirectory.nativePath + "\n\n";
                          s += "File.applicationStorageDirectory : " +
                              File.applicationStorageDirectory.nativePath + "\n\n";
                          s += "File.desktopDirectory: " +
                              File.desktopDirectory.nativePath + "\n\n";
                          s += "File.documentsDirectory : " +
                              File.documentsDirectory.nativePath + "\n\n";
                          s += "File.userDirectory : " +
                              File.userDirectory.nativePath + "\n\n";
                          info.text = s;
                  }

          ]]>
      </fx:Script>
      <fx:Declarations>
              <!-- Place non-visual elements (e.g., services, value objects) here -->
      </fx:Declarations>

      <s:Label text="File System Paths" top="10" width="100%" textAlign="center"/>

      <s:TextArea id="info" width="100%" height="100%" top="40" editable="false"/>

  </s:Application>
```

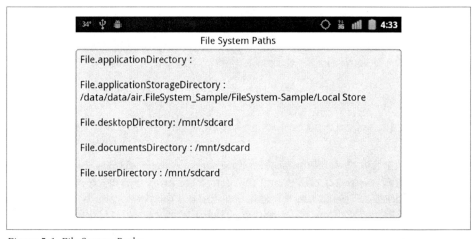

Figure 5-1. File System Paths

Read and Write to the File System

Adobe AIR provides you with the ability to read and write files to the file system. The following example will create a new file and then read it back.

Let's review the code below. There are two TextArea and two Button components that make up this sample. The first TextArea (with an id of contents) will hold the contents of what is to be written to the file. The second (with an id of results) will output the file contents when read back. The application can be seen in Figure 5-2.

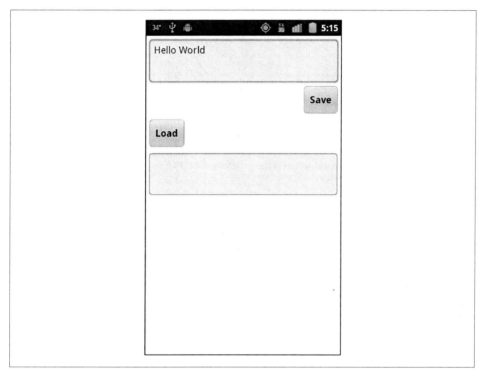

Figure 5-2. The File Save application

Clicking on the Button labeled Save will call the button1_clickHandler method. Within the button1_clickHandler method, an instance of File is created with the name file, the path is resolved to the userDirectory, and "samples/test.txt" is passed in to the resolvePath method. An instance of FileStream named stream is created to write the data to the file. The open method is then called on the stream object, and the file and FileMode.WRITE are passed in, which will open the file with write permissions. Next, the writeUTFBytes method is called and contents.text is passed in. Finally, the stream is closed. Figure 5-3 shows the new file within the File Manager application after it has been created.

Clicking on the `Button` labeled `Load` will call the `button2_clickHandler` method. Within the `button2_clickHandler` method, an instance of `File` is created with the name `file`, the path is resolved to the `userDirectory`, and `"samples/test.txt"` is passed in to the `resolvePath` method. An instance of `FileStream` named `stream` is created to read the data from the file. The `open` method is called on the `stream` object, and the file and `FileMode.READ` are passed in, which will open the file with write permissions. Next, the `readUTFBytes` method is called, the `stream.bytesAvailable` is passed in, and the results are set to the `results.text` property of the second `TextArea`. Finally, the stream is closed. Figure 5-4 shows the contents of the file within the `results` TextArea:

```
<?xml version="1.0" encoding="utf-8"?>
<s:Application xmlns:fx="http://ns.adobe.com/mxml/2009"
               xmlns:s="library://ns.adobe.com/flex/spark">

    <fx:Script>
        <![CDATA[

            protectedfunction button1_clickHandler(event:MouseEvent):void
            {
                var file:File = File.userDirectory.resolvePath
                    ("samples/test.txt");
                var stream:FileStream = new FileStream()
                stream.open(file, FileMode.WRITE);
                stream.writeUTFBytes(contents.text);
                stream.close();
            }

            protectedfunction button2_clickHandler(event:MouseEvent):void
            {
                var file:File = File.userDirectory.resolvePath
                    ("samples/test.txt");
                varstream:FileStream = new FileStream()
                stream.open(file, FileMode.READ);
                results.text = stream.readUTFBytes(stream.bytesAvailable);
                stream.close();
            }

        ]]>
    </fx:Script>

    <fx:Declarations>
        <!-- Place non-visual elements (e.g., services, value objects) here -->
    </fx:Declarations>

    <s:TextArea id="contents" left="10" right="10" top="10" height="100"/>
    <s:Button right="10" top="120" label="Save" click="button1_clickHandler(event)"/>

    <s:Button left="10" top="200" label="Load" click="button2_clickHandler(event)"/>
    <s:TextArea id="results" left="10" right="10" top="280" height="100"
        editable="false"/>
</s:Application>
```

Figure 5-3. A new file shown within File Manager

Figure 5-4. File contents loaded into the results TextArea

File Browse for a Single File

The browse for file functionality of the File class works a bit differently in Android as compared to the desktop. Within Android, the browseForOpen method will open up a specific native file selector that will allow you to open a file of type *Audio*, *Image*, or *Video*.

Let's review the code below. The Button with the Browse label will call the button1_click Handler when clicked. Within this function, an instance of File is created with the variable name file. An event listener is added for Event.SELECT with the responding method of onFileSelect, and the browseForOpen method is called. The application can be seen in Figure 5-5. When browseForOpen is called, the Android file selector is launched. This can be seen in Figure 5-6. After selecting a file within the Android file selector, the event is fired and the onFileSelect method is called. The event.current Target is cast to a File object, and its nativePath, extension, and url properties are used to display the nativePath and the image in the example (shown in Figure 5-7):

```
<?xml version="1.0" encoding="utf-8"?>
<s:Application xmlns:fx="http://ns.adobe.com/mxml/2009"
               xmlns:s="library://ns.adobe.com/flex/spark">

    <fx:Script>
        <![CDATA[

            protectedfunction button1_clickHandler(event:MouseEvent):void
            {
                var file:File = new File();
                file.addEventListener(Event.SELECT, onFileSelect);
                file.browseForOpen("Open");
            }

            privatefunction onFileSelect(event:Event):void {
                var file:File = File(event.currentTarget);
                filepath.text = file.nativePath;
                if(file.extension == "jpg"){
                    image.source = file.url;
                }
            }
        ]]>
    </fx:Script>

    <fx:Declarations>
        <!-- Place non-visual elements (e.g., services, value objects) here -->
    </fx:Declarations>

    <s:Button horizontalCenter="0" top="10" label="Browse"
        click="button1_clickHandler(event)"/>
    <s:Label id="filepath" left="10" right="10" top="100"/>
    <s:Image id="image" width="230" height="350" top="150" horizontalCenter="0"/>
</s:Application>
```

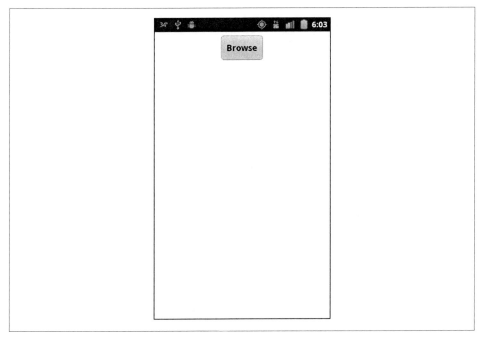

Figure 5-5. The Browse for File application

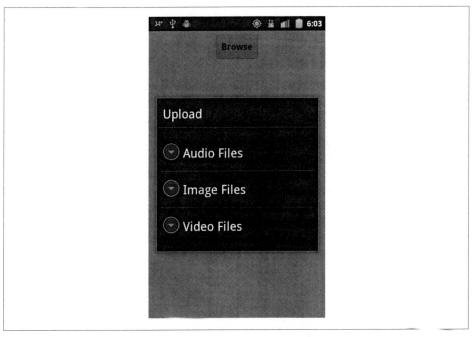

Figure 5-6. The file selector

Figure 5-7. The Browse for File application with an image selected

File Browse for Multiple Files

Within Android, the browseForOpenMultiple method will open up a specific native file selector that will allow you to open multiple files of type Audio, Image, or Video.

Let's review the code below. The Button with the Browse label will call the button1_click Handler when clicked. Within this function, an instance of File is created with the variable name file. An event listener is added for FileListEvent.SELECT_MULTIPLE with the responding method of onMultipleFileSelect, and the browseForOpen method is called. When browseForOpen is called, the Android file selector is launched. This can be seen in Figure 5-8. After selecting the files within the Android file selector, the event is fired and the onMultipleFileSelect method is called. Within this method, the array of files included in the event is looped over—and if the file type is an image, it is added as a new element. The results can be seen in Figure 5-9:

```
<?xml version="1.0" encoding="utf-8"?>
<s:Application xmlns:fx="http://ns.adobe.com/mxml/2009"
               xmlns:s="library://ns.adobe.com/flex/spark">

    <fx:Script>
        <![CDATA[
            import spark.components.Image;

            protectedfunction button1_clickHandler(event:MouseEvent):void
            {
                var file:File = new File();
                file.addEventListener(FileListEvent.SELECT_MULTIPLE,
                    onMultipleFileSelect);
                file.browseForOpenMultiple("Open");
            }

            privatefunction onMultipleFileSelect(event:FileListEvent):void {
                holder.removeAllElements();
                for (var i:int=0; i<event.files.length; i++){
                    var f:File = event.files[i] as File;
                    if(f.extension == "jpg"){
                        var image:Image = new Image();
                        image.source = f.url;
                        image.scaleX = .1;
                        image.scaleY = .1;
                        holder.addElement(image);
                    }
                }
            }
        ]]>
    </fx:Script>

    <fx:Declarations>
        <!-- Place non-visual elements (e.g., services, value objects) here -->
    </fx:Declarations>

    <s:Button horizontalCenter="0" top="10" label="Browse" click=
        "button1_clickHandler(event)"/>
    <s:Label id="filepath" left="10" right="10" top="100"/>
    <s:Scroller top="150" horizontalCenter="0" bottom="0">
        <s:VGroup id="holder"/>
    </s:Scroller>

</s:Application>
```

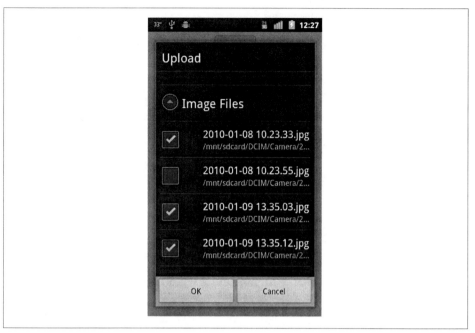

Figure 5-8. Browse for multiple files

Figure 5-9. Multiple images selected

SQLite Databases

Just as with Adobe AIR on the desktop, you can use an SQLite database to store data on a mobile device. The example below will create a database, use a simple form to save data to that database, and retrieve and display the stored data.

Let's review the code below. At the top, you will see the database file defined as a file called *users.db* within the userDirectory. Next, the SQLConnection is defined. Finally, there are several SQLStatements declared and SQL strings defined, which will be used for working with the database.

Within the applicationComplete event handler, the SQLConnection is initiated; two event listeners are added to listen for SQLEvent.OPEN and SQLErrorEvent.ERROR; and finally, the openAsync method is called and the *db* file is passed in.

After the database is opened, the openHandler function is called. Within this function, the SQLEvent.OPEN event listener is removed. Next, createTableStmt is created, configured, and executed. This statement will create a new table called Users (if it doesn't yet exist). If it is successful, then the createResult method is called. Within the create Result method, the SQLEvent.RESULT event is removed and the selectUsers method is called.

Within the selectUsers method, selectStmt is created, configured, and executed. This statement will return all rows within the Users table. This data is then stored within the selectStmt. If it is successful, the selectResult method is called. Within the selectResult method, the data is read from the selectStmt using the getResults method. It is then cast to an ArrayCollection and set to the dataProvider of a DataGroup, where it is shown on screen by formatting within an itemRenderer named UserRenderer.

All of the processes just described occur as chained events when the application loads up. So if there is any data in the database from previous uses, it will automatically display when the application is loaded. This can be seen in Figure 5-10.

The only remaining functionality is the ability to add a new user. There are two text fields with the ids of firstName and lastName, and a Button that when clicked will call the button1_clickHandler function. Within the button1_clickHandler function, insertStmt is created, configured, and executed. Notice that within the insertStmt configuration, the parameters firstName and lastName (which were defined in insertSQL) are set to the text properties of the firstName and lastName TextInput components. If it is successful, the insertResult method is called. Within the insert Result method, the selectUsers method is called and the DataGroup is updated, showing the newly-added data. This can be seen in Figure 5-11.

Here is the code for the main application:

```
<?xml version="1.0" encoding="utf-8"?>
<s:Application xmlns:fx="http://ns.adobe.com/mxml/2009"
               xmlns:s="library://ns.adobe.com/flex/spark"
               applicationComplete=
                   "application1_applicationCompleteHandler(event)">
    <fx:Script>
        <![CDATA[
            import mx.collections.ArrayCollection;
            import mx.events.FlexEvent;

            privatevar db:File = File.userDirectory.resolvePath("users.db");
            privatevar conn:SQLConnection;

            privatevar createTableStmt:SQLStatement;
            privatevar createTableSQL:String =
                "CREATE TABLE IF NOT EXISTS User (" +
                    "userId INTEGER PRIMARY KEY AUTOINCREMENT," +
                    "firstName TEXT," + "lastName TEXT)";

            privatevar selectStmt:SQLStatement;
            privatevar selectSQL:String = "SELECT * FROM User";

            privatevar insertStmt:SQLStatement;
            privatevar insertSQL:String =
                "INSERT INTO User (firstName, lastName)" +
                    "VALUES (:firstName, :lastName)";

            protectedfunction application1_applicationCompleteHandler
                (event:FlexEvent):void
            {
                conn = new SQLConnection();
                conn.addEventListener(SQLEvent.OPEN, openHandler);
                conn.addEventListener(SQLErrorEvent.ERROR, errorHandler);
                conn.openAsync(db);
            }

            privatefunction openHandler(event:SQLEvent):void {
                log.text += "Database opened successfully";
                conn.removeEventListener(SQLEvent.OPEN, openHandler);
                createTableStmt = new SQLStatement();
                createTableStmt.sqlConnection = conn;
                createTableStmt.text = createTableSQL;
                createTableStmt.addEventListener(SQLEvent.RESULT, createResult);
                createTableStmt.addEventListener(SQLErrorEvent.ERROR,
                    errorHandler);
                createTableStmt.execute();
            }

            privatefunction createResult(event:SQLEvent):void {
                log.text += "\nTable created";
                conn.removeEventListener(SQLEvent.RESULT, createResult);
                selectUsers();
            }
```

```
            privatefunction errorHandler(event:SQLErrorEvent):void {
                    log.text += "\nError message: " + event.error.message;
                    log.text += "\nDetails: " + event.error.details;
            }

            privatefunction selectUsers():void{
                    selectStmt = new SQLStatement();
                    selectStmt.sqlConnection = conn;
                    selectStmt.text = selectSQL;
                    selectStmt.addEventListener(SQLEvent.RESULT, selectResult);
                    selectStmt.addEventListener(SQLErrorEvent.ERROR, errorHandler);
                    selectStmt.execute();
            }

            privatefunction selectResult(event:SQLEvent):void {
                    log.text += "\nSelect completed";
                    var result:SQLResult = selectStmt.getResult();
                    users.dataProvider = new ArrayCollection(result.data);
            }

            protectedfunction button1_clickHandler(event:MouseEvent):void
            {
                    insertStmt = new SQLStatement();
                    insertStmt.sqlConnection = conn;
                    insertStmt.text = insertSQL;
                    insertStmt.parameters[":firstName"] = firstName.text;
                    insertStmt.parameters[":lastName"] = lastName.text;
                    insertStmt.addEventListener(SQLEvent.RESULT, insertResult);
                    insertStmt.addEventListener(SQLErrorEvent.ERROR, errorHandler);
                    insertStmt.execute();
            }

            privatefunction insertResult(event:SQLEvent):void {
                    log.text += "\nInsert completed";
                    selectUsers();
            }

        ]]>
</fx:Script>
<fx:Declarations>
        <!-- Place non-visual elements (e.g., services, value objects) here -->
</fx:Declarations>

<s:Label text="First name" top="35" left="10"/>
<s:TextInput id="firstName" left="150" top="10" width="300"/>

<s:Label text="Last name" top="95" left="10"/>
<s:TextInput id="lastName" left="150" top="70" width="300"/>

<s:Button label="Save" click="button1_clickHandler(event)" top="130" left="150"/>

<s:Scroller height="200" width="100%" left="10" right="10" top="200">
        <s:DataGroup id="users" height="100%" width="95%"
                        itemRenderer="UserRenderer">
```

```
            <s:layout>
                    <s:VerticalLayout/>
            </s:layout>
        </s:DataGroup>
    </s:Scroller>

    <s:TextArea id="log" width="100%" bottom="0" height="250"/>

</s:Application>
```

The code for the UserRenderer:

```
<?xml version="1.0" encoding="utf-8"?>
<s:ItemRenderer xmlns:fx="http://ns.adobe.com/mxml/2009"
                    xmlns:s="library://ns.adobe.com/flex/spark">
    <s:Label text="{data.lastName}, {data.firstName}"/>
</s:ItemRenderer>
```

Figure 5-10. SQLite sample application

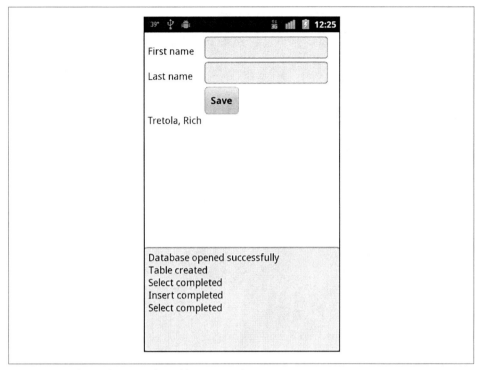

Figure 5-11. The application after adding a record

CHAPTER 6

OS Interactions

Open in Browser

From within your application, you can open a link using the device's native browser in the same manner as you would in a traditional browser-based Flex application. This is accomplished with the URLRequest class. Simply creating a new URLRequest and passing it into the navigateToURL method will invoke the user's browser to handle the request. Figure 6-1 shows the sample application running and Figure 6-2 shows the results of clicking on the Open button:

```
<?xml version="1.0" encoding="utf-8"?>
<s:Application xmlns:fx="http://ns.adobe.com/mxml/2009"
               xmlns:s="library://ns.adobe.com/flex/spark">

    <fx:Script>
        <![CDATA[
            protectedfunction sendIt_clickHandler(event:MouseEvent):void
            {
                var s:String = "";
                s+= address.text;
                navigateToURL(new URLRequest(s));

            }
        ]]>
    </fx:Script>

    <fx:Declarations>
        <!-- Place non-visual elements (e.g., services, value objects) here -->
    </fx:Declarations>

    <s:Label text="URL" top="40" left="50"/>
    <s:TextInput id="address" top="30" left="160" text="http://www.happytoad.com"
        width="250"/>
    <s:Button id="sendIt" label="Open" click="sendIt_clickHandler(event)" top="110"
        left="160"/>
</s:Application>
```

Figure 6-1. Open a link in a browser

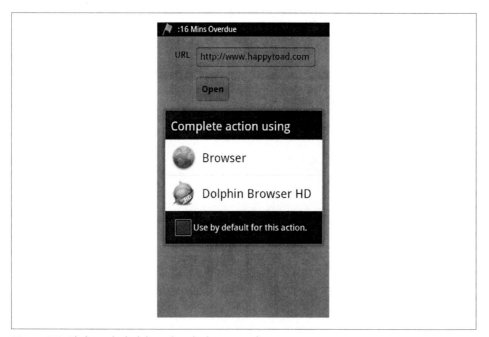

Figure 6-2. Clicking the link launches the browser selector

Create Text Message

The URLRequest class can be used to open the Messaging application to send text messages. By prepending the request with sms:, you will tell Android to launch the Messaging application when the navigateToURL method is called. Figure 6-3 shows the sample application running and Figure 6-4 shows the Messaging application with the phone number pre-populated. Unfortunately, at this time it is not possible to send a message along with the phone number when using the Messaging application:

```
<?xml version="1.0" encoding="utf-8"?>
<s:Application xmlns:fx="http://ns.adobe.com/mxml/2009"
               xmlns:s="library://ns.adobe.com/flex/spark">

    <fx:Script>
        <![CDATA[
            protectedfunction sendIt_clickHandler(event:MouseEvent):void
            {
                var s:String = "";
                s += "sms:";
                s+= sendTo.text;
                navigateToURL(new URLRequest(s));

            }
        ]]>
    </fx:Script>

    <fx:Declarations>
        <!-- Place non-visual elements (e.g., services, value objects) here -->
    </fx:Declarations>

    <s:Label text="Send To" top="40" left="50"/>
    <s:TextInput id="sendTo" top="30" left="160" text="2125559999" width="250"/>
    <s:Button id="sendIt" label="Send" click="sendIt_clickHandler(event)" top="110"
        left="160"/>
</s:Application>
```

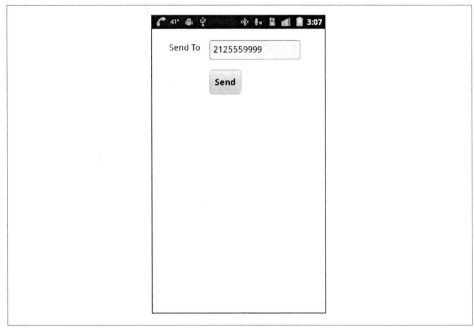

Figure 6-3. Open a text message in the Messaging application

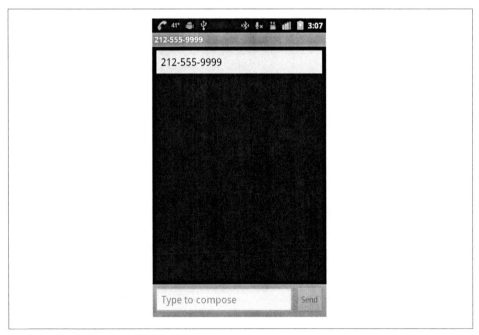

Figure 6-4. The Messenging application has opened

Create Email

The `URLRequest` class can be used to open the Messaging application to send text messages. By prepending the request with `mailto:`, you will tell Android to launch the Email application when the `navigateToURL` method is called. There are several properties that can be passed into the `URLRequest` to set the "send to" email address, the email subject, and the email message.

Figure 6-5 shows the sample application running, Figure 6-6 shows the email selection window being launched after the Send button has been clicked, and Figure 6-7 shows the properties being pre-populated in the Gmail application:

```
<?xml version="1.0" encoding="utf-8"?>
<s:Application xmlns:fx="http://ns.adobe.com/mxml/2009"
               xmlns:s="library://ns.adobe.com/flex/spark">

    <fx:Script>
        <![CDATA[
            protectedfunction sendIt_clickHandler(event:MouseEvent):void
            {
                vars:String = "";
                s += "mailto:";
                s+= sendTo.text;
                s+= "?";
                s+= "subject=";
                s+= subject.text;
                s+= "&";
                s+= "body=";
                s+= message.text;
                navigateToURL(new URLRequest(s));

            }
        ]]>
    </fx:Script>

    <fx:Declarations>
        <!-- Place non-visual elements (e.g., services, value objects) here -->
    </fx:Declarations>

    <s:Label text="Send To" top="40" left="50"/>
    <s:TextInput id="sendTo" top="30" left="160" text="rtretola@gmail.com"
        width="250"/>
    <s:Label text="Subject" top="100" left="50"/>
    <s:TextInput id="subject" top="90" left="160" text="hello" width="250"/>
    <s:Label text="Message" top="160" left="50"/>
    <s:TextInput id="message" top="150" left="160" width="250"/>
    <s:Button id="sendIt" label="Send" click="sendIt_clickHandler(event)" top="210"
        left="160"/>
</s:Application>
```

Figure 6-5. A sample Email application

Figure 6-6. The email selector after clicking Send

Figure 6-7. Message properties set within Gmail

Place Call

The `URLRequest` class can be used to open the Phone application to place a call. By prepending the request with `tel:`, you will tell Android to launch the Phone application when the `navigateToURL` method is called. Figure 6-8 shows the sample application running and Figure 6-9 shows the Phone application with the phone number pre-populated:

```
<?xml version="1.0" encoding="utf-8"?>
<s:Application xmlns:fx="http://ns.adobe.com/mxml/2009"
               xmlns:s="library://ns.adobe.com/flex/spark">

    <fx:Script>
        <![CDATA[
            protectedfunction sendIt_clickHandler(event:MouseEvent):void
            {
                var s:String = "";
                s += "tel:";
                s+= call.text;
                navigateToURL(new URLRequest(s));

            }
        ]]>
```

```
    </fx:Script>

    <fx:Declarations>
        <!-- Place non-visual elements (e.g., services, value objects) here -->
    </fx:Declarations>

    <s:Label text="Phone #" top="40" left="50"/>
    <s:TextInput id="call" top="30" left="160" text="2125559999" width="250"/>
    <s:Button id="sendIt" label="Send" click="sendIt_clickHandler(event)" top="110"
        left="160"/>
</s:Application>
```

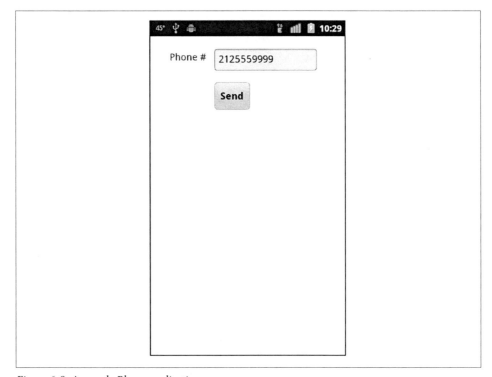

Figure 6-8. A sample Phone application

Figure 6-9. The Phone application with number pre-populated

Splash Screen

Adobe has made it very easy to add a splash screen to your application. A splash screen is an image that loads first and displays while the application is loading. There are several options for the display of this splash screen, but let's look at a basic sample, which shows the splashScreenImage property being set to a *.png* image. Figure 6-10 shows a splash screen with the default settings:

```
<?xml version="1.0" encoding="utf-8"?>
<s:Application xmlns:fx="http://ns.adobe.com/mxml/2009"
               xmlns:s="library://ns.adobe.com/flex/spark"
               splashScreenImage="@Embed('happytoad.png')">
    <fx:Declarations>
        <!-- Place non-visual elements (e.g., services, value objects) here -->
    </fx:Declarations>
</s:Application>
```

Figure 6-10. Splash screen with splashScreenScaleMode set to none

There are also some options that can be set on the splash screen. Applying the `splash ScreenMinimumDisplayTime` and `splashScreenScaleMode` properties to the `Application`, `ViewNavigatorApplication`, or `TabbedViewNavigatorApplication` tags sets these options. The example below sets the display time to 3 seconds and the scale mode to stretch.

The available options for the `splashScreenScaleMode` property are `letterbox`, `none`, `stretch`, and `zoom`. Figure 6-11 shows a splash screen with the `splashScreenScaleMode` set to `stretch`:

```
<?xml version="1.0" encoding="utf-8"?>
<s:Application xmlns:fx="http://ns.adobe.com/mxml/2009"
               xmlns:s="library://ns.adobe.com/flex/spark"
               splashScreenImage="@Embed('happytoad.png')"
               splashScreenMinimumDisplayTime="3000"
            splashScreenScaleMode="stretch">
    <fx:Declarations>
        <!-- Place non-visual elements (e.g., services, value objects) here -->
    </fx:Declarations>
</s:Application>
```

Figure 6-11. Splash screen with splashScreenScaleMode set to stretch

StageWebView

The StageWebView allows for web (HTML and Flash on supported devices) and video content to be loaded into a Flex application. StageWebView will utilize the native browser to load HTML into your application.

Let's review the code below. First, you will notice there is a private variable named stageWebView declared, of type flash.media.StageWebView. Within application Complete of the application, an event handler function is called, which first checks to see if the device supports StageWebView by reading the static property of the StageWeb View class. If this property returns as true, a new instance of StageWebView and a new Rectangle (sized to fill the remaining screen and set to the viewport property of the stageWebView) are created.

There is a TextInput component with the id of urlAddress, which holds the address that will be shown in the StageWebView and a Button labeled GO.

Clicking on the GO button will call the button1_clickHandler method. Within the but ton1_clickHandler method, the loadURL method is called with the urlAddress.text property passed in. This triggers the StageWebView to load the URL.

The results can be seen within Figure 6-12:

```xml
<?xml version="1.0" encoding="utf-8"?>
<s:Application xmlns:fx="http://ns.adobe.com/mxml/2009"
               xmlns:s="library://ns.adobe.com/flex/spark"
               applicationComplete=
                   "application1_applicationCompleteHandler(event)">
    <fx:Script>
        <![CDATA[
            import mx.events.FlexEvent;

            privatevar stageWebView:StageWebView;
            privatevar rect:Rectangle;

            protectedfunction application1_applicationCompleteHandler
                (event:FlexEvent):void
            {
                if(StageWebView.isSupported==true){
                    stageWebView = new StagewebView();
                    stageWebView.viewPort = new Rectangle(5,80,stage.width-10,
                        stage.height-90);
                    stageWebView.stage = this.stage;
                } else {
                    urlAddress.text = "StageWebView not supported";
                }
            }

            protectedfunction button1_clickHandler(event:MouseEvent):void
            {
                stageWebView.loadURL(urlAddress.text);
            }

        ]]>
    </fx:Script>
    <fx:Declarations>
        <!-- Place non-visual elements (e.g., services, value objects) here -->
    </fx:Declarations>

    <s:TextInput id="urlAddress" left="5" right="80" top="15"
        text="http://www.google.com"/>
    <s:Button right="5" top="5" label="GO" click="button1_clickHandler(event)"/>

</s:Application>
```

Figure 6-12. StageWebView with the Google homepage loaded

Screen Options

There are several options available to programmatically control several areas of the screen layout. These options include the layout of the application; whether or not to show the action bar in View-Based or Tabbed Applications; and whether or not to show the application in full screen mode. A sample application can be seen in Figure 6-13.

Layout

The options for your application layout are portrait (where the application is displayed vertically on the device) or landscape (where the application is displayed horizontally). Setting the aspect ratio by calling the setAspectRatio method on the stage can change the application's layout. The StageAspectRatio class contains two static values that should be used to set the aspect ratio.

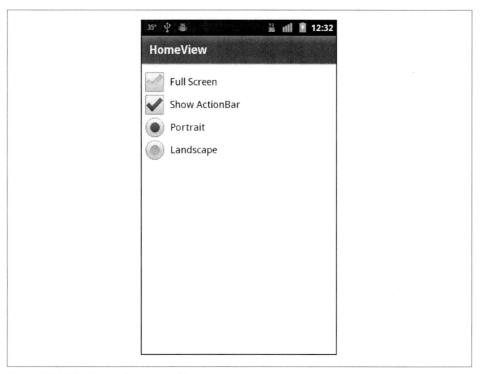

Figure 6-13. The Screen Options application

The code below includes a RadioGroup with the id of orientation. There are two RadioButton components in this group, with values of portrait and landscape. When clicking on one of these radio buttons, the radiobutton1_clickHandler method is called. Within this method, the orientation.selectedValue is tested. If orientation.selected Value is equal to portrait, the stage.setAspectRatio method is called and StageAspec tRatio.PORTRAIT is passed in. If orientation.selectedValue is equal to landscape, the stage.setAspectRatio method is called and StageAspectRatio.LANDSCAPE is passed in. The results can be seen in Figure 6-14.

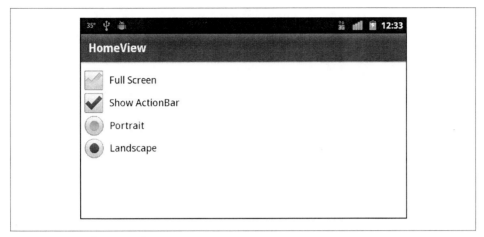

Figure 6-14. Landscape mode

Full Screen

Utilizing the entire screen for your mobile application is an option that you can set within your application, and there are a few choices when this change is requested. To put an application in full screen mode, you will need to set the displayState property on the stage. There are several static properties within the StageDisplayState class that can be used for this.

The code below includes a CheckBox with the label "FullScreen". This CheckBox is not selected by default, as that is the normal state of the application. When clicking on this CheckBox to check or uncheck the value, the checkbox1_clickHandler is called. If the checkbox is checked, the stage.displayState is set to StageDisplayState. FULL_SCREEN_INTERACTIVE. If the checkbox is not checked, the stage.displayState is set to StageDisplayState.NORMAL.

> The StageDisplayState also has a static property of StageDisplay State.FULL_SCREEN. This property can be used to put the application in full screen mode when the keyboard is unnecessary. The results can be seen in Figure 6-15.

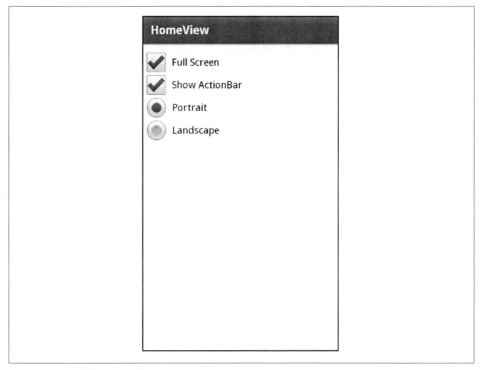

Figure 6-15. Full Screen mode

ActionBar

The *ActionBar* is the built-in navigation system that comes along with the View-Based or Tabbed Application layouts. This bar does consume significant screen real estate. Therefore, the option to hide and show this bar programmatically is available to you as the developer.

The code below includes a CheckBox with the label "Show ActionBar". This CheckBox is selected by default, as that is the normal state of the ActionBar. When clicking on this CheckBox to check or uncheck the value, the checkbox2_clickHandler is called. The actionBarVisible property of this View is set to the value of the CheckBox. The results can be seen in Figure 6-16, which shows a full screen application with the ActionBar hidden:

```
<?xml version="1.0" encoding="utf-8"?>
<s:View xmlns:fx="http://ns.adobe.com/mxml/2009"
        xmlns:s="library://ns.adobe.com/flex/spark" title="HomeView">
```

```
<fx:Script>
    <![CDATA[
        protectedfunction checkbox1_clickHandler(event:MouseEvent):void
        {
            if(event.target.selected){
                stage.displayState =
                    StageDisplayState.FULL_SCREEN_INTERACTIVE;
            } else {
                stage.displayState = StageDisplayState.NORMAL;
            }
        }

        protectedfunction checkbox2_clickHandler(event:MouseEvent):void
        {
            this.actionBarVisible = event.target.selected;
        }

        protectedfunctionradiobutton1_clickHandler(event:MouseEvent):void
        {
            if(orientation.selectedValue == "portrait"){
                stage.setAspectRatio(StageAspectRatio.PORTRAIT);
            } elseif(orientation.selectedValue == "landscape"){
                stage.setAspectRatio(StageAspectRatio.LANDSCAPE);
            }
        }

    ]]>
</fx:Script>

<fx:Declarations>
    <s:RadioButtonGroup id="orientation"/>
</fx:Declarations>

<s:VGroup top="20" left="10">
    <s:CheckBox click="checkbox1_clickHandler(event)" label="Full Screen"/>
    <s:CheckBox click="checkbox2_clickHandler(event)" label="Show ActionBar"
            selected="true"/>
    <s:RadioButton groupName="orientation" value="portrait" label="Portrait"
                click="radiobutton1_clickHandler(event)"
                    selected="true"/>
    <s:RadioButton groupName="orientation" value="landscape" label="Landscape"
                click="radiobutton1_clickHandler(event)"/>
</s:VGroup>


</s:View>
```

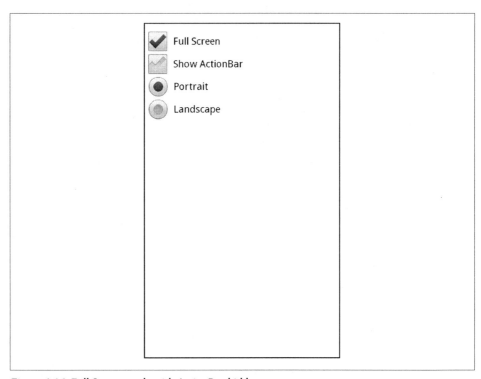

Figure 6-16. Full Screen mode with ActionBar hidden

CHAPTER 7

Publish to Android Installer

Now that you have created your new application, it is time to publish it to an Android installer file, which is an archive file with an *.apk* extension. Flash Builder provides all of the tools to accomplish this task.

To demonstrate how to compile an application to an Android installer, let's walk through this process with the following steps:

1. First, click on File→Export within Flash Builder's main menu (see Figure 7-1).

2. Next, select Flash Builder→Release Build (see Figure 7-2).

3. Within the Export Release Build window, select the Project and Application that you would like to compile (see Figure 7-3).

4. If you already have a certificate compiled, select that certificate, enter its password, and click the Finish button to compile the Android installer file (*.apk*). If you do not yet have a certificate, click the Create button (see Figure 7-4).

   To create a new certificate, complete the Create Self-Signed Digital Certificate form and click on the OK button (see Figure 7-5).

5. To compile the Android installer file (*.apk*), click on the Finish button (see Figure 7-6).

Congratulations: you have just compiled your first Android application. To publish your new application to the Android Market, just visit *https://market.android .com/publish*.

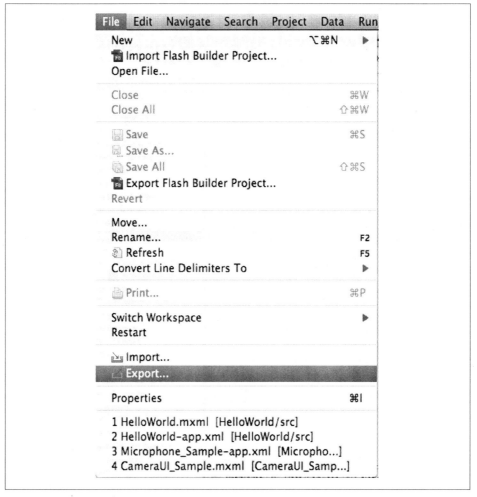

Figure 7-1. Selecting File→Export

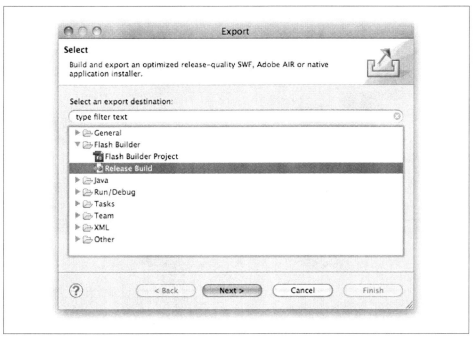

Figure 7-2. Selecting Flash Builder→Release Build

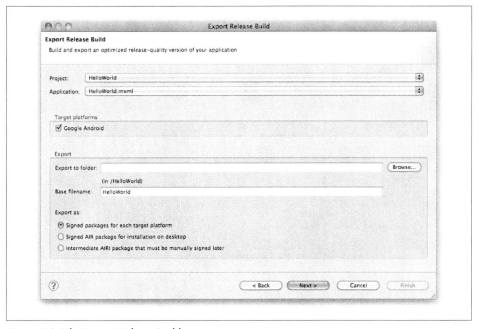

Figure 7-3. The Export Release Build screen

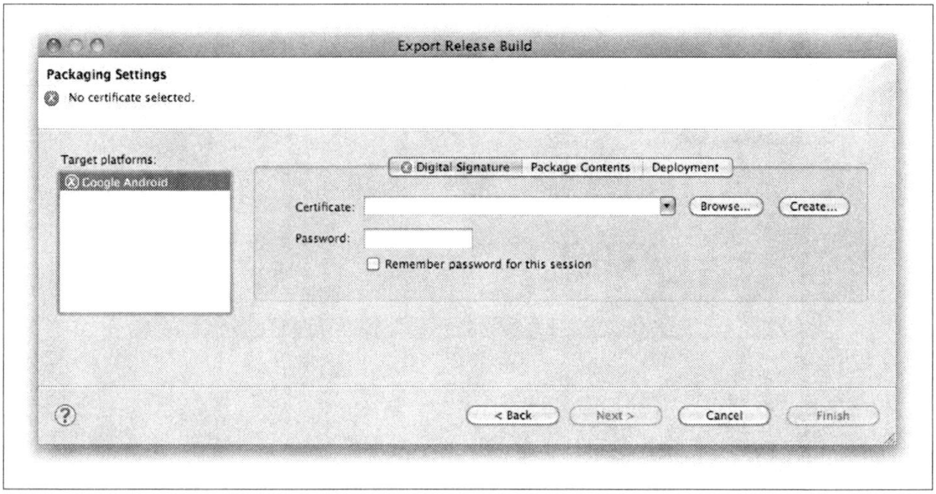

Figure 7-4. Selecting or creating a certificate

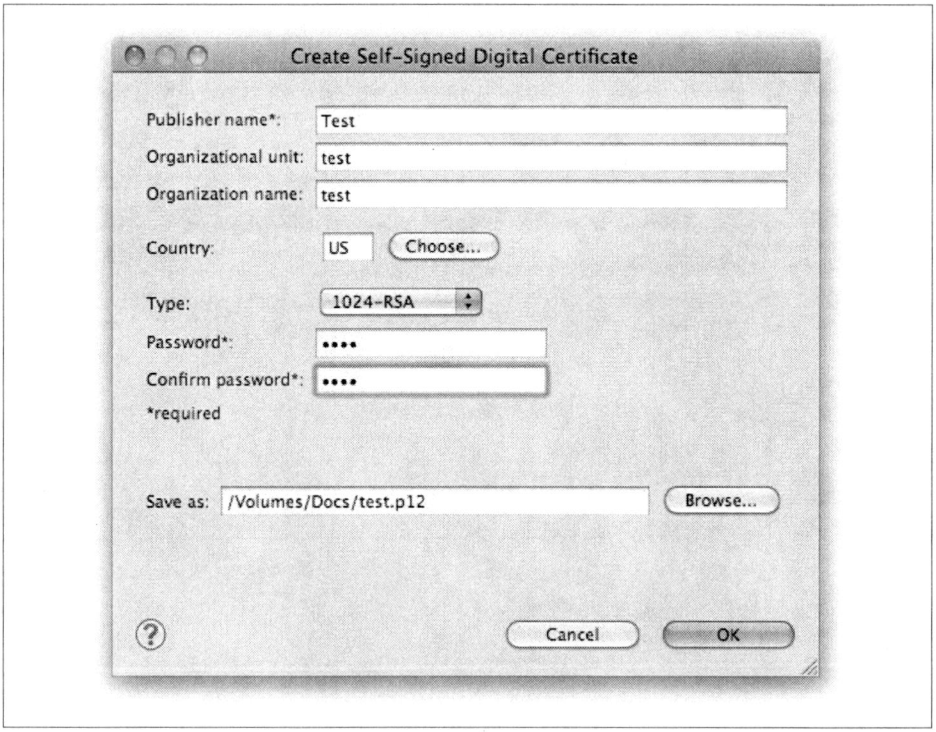

Figure 7-5. Creating a new certificate

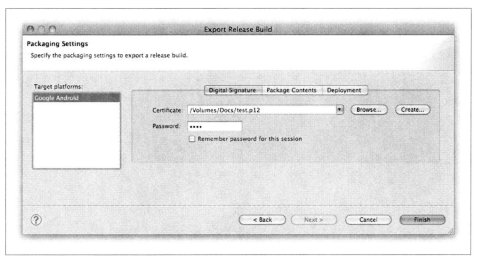

Figure 7-6. Completing the export

About the Author

Rich Tretola, an award-winning Flex developer, is the Applications Development Manager at Herff Jones Inc. He has been building Internet applications for over a decade, and has worked with Flex since the original Royale beta was introduced in 2003. Outside of Flex, Rich builds applications using ColdFusion, Flash, and Java. He is highly regarded in the Flex community as an expert in RIA, and is also a five-time Adobe Community Professional.

He is the lead author of Professional Flex 2 (Wrox) and sole author of Beginning AIR (Wrox). He is also a contributing author on Adobe AIR 1.5 Cookbook (O'Reilly) and Flex 4 Cookbook (O'Reilly). He runs a popular Flex and AIR blog at Everything-Flex.com, was the community manager of InsideRIA.com for over three years, and has also been a speaker at over 10 Adobe MAX sessions.

Recently, Rich has re-engaged the RIA development community by founding RIARockStars.com, and has been a principal partner in a new social polling service at twittapolls.com. For a non-technical escape, Rich is also a co-owner of a chocolate company in Hawaii named WowWee Maui (*http://www.wowweemaui.com*).

Get even more for your money.

Join the O'Reilly Community, and register the O'Reilly books you own. It's free, and you'll get:

- $4.99 ebook upgrade offer
- 40% upgrade offer on O'Reilly print books
- Membership discounts on books and events
- Free lifetime updates to ebooks and videos
- Multiple ebook formats, DRM FREE
- Participation in the O'Reilly community
- Newsletters
- Account management
- 100% Satisfaction Guarantee

Signing up is easy:

1. **Go to: oreilly.com/go/register**
2. **Create an O'Reilly login.**
3. **Provide your address.**
4. **Register your books.**

Note: English-language books only

To order books online:
oreilly.com/store

For questions about products or an order:
orders@oreilly.com

To sign up to get topic-specific email announcements and/or news about upcoming books, conferences, special offers, and new technologies:
elists@oreilly.com

For technical questions about book content:
booktech@oreilly.com

To submit new book proposals to our editors:
proposals@oreilly.com

O'Reilly books are available in multiple DRM-free ebook formats. For more information:
oreilly.com/ebooks

O'REILLY®

The information you need, when and where you need it.

With Safari Books Online, you can:

Access the contents of thousands of technology and business books

- Quickly search over 7000 books and certification guides
- Download whole books or chapters in PDF format, at no extra cost, to print or read on the go
- Copy and paste code
- Save up to 35% on O'Reilly print books
- **New!** Access mobile-friendly books directly from cell phones and mobile devices

Stay up-to-date on emerging topics before the books are published

- Get on-demand access to evolving manuscripts.
- Interact directly with authors of upcoming books

Explore thousands of hours of video on technology and design topics

- Learn from expert video tutorials
- Watch and replay recorded conference sessions

CPSIA information can be obtained at www.ICGtesting.com
Printed in the USA
266748BV00009B/7/P